A PLEA FOR PURITY

A PLEA FOR
PURITY

SEX, MARRIAGE & GOD

JOHANN CHRISTOPH ARNOLD

 PLOUGH PUBLISHING HOUSE

Farmington, PA 15437, U.S.A.
Robertsbridge, East Sussex TN32 5DR, U.K.

First Printing   6,000   April 1996

Library of Congress Cataloging-in-Publication Data

Arnold, J.Christoph (Johann Christoph), 1940–
   A plea for purity: sex, marriage, and God / J. Christoph Arnold ;
foreword by Mother Teresa.
      p.   cm.
   Includes bibliographical references.
   ISBN 0-87486-072-5 (pbk.)
      1. Sex – Religious aspects – Christianity.   2. Sex – Religious aspects –
Bruderhof Communities.   3. Marriage – Religious aspects – Christianity.
4. Marriage – Religious aspects – Bruderhof Communities.   5. Bruderhof
Communities – Doctrines.   I. Title.
   BV708.A75 1996
   248.4 – dc20   95–52528
                                                                        CIP
   Printed in USA

TO THE READER

When I began reading the manuscript for *A Plea for Purity* – the book you're holding – my first reaction was anger. I felt as if someone was condemning and virtually tearing apart every morsel of my life. How could someone who had not walked in my shoes do that? Maybe the perfect Christian relationship or marriage could belong to someone who lived in the confines of some devout community, I thought – but that ideal was never available to me. Both my parents have divorced and remarried more than once, and I'm expecting a child by a man I'm not married to. I live in reality.

During many nights of reading I'd become so upset that I needed to put the book down. At one point I even told myself I wouldn't continue. Then someone advised me to read the gospels and see what they had to say about love and marriage – not as a fact-finding mission, but as a means of spiritual seeking. On reading the gospels with their message of hope, I decided that I needed to re-evaluate my attitude toward the book.

When I returned to the beginning of the book and started to read it again, I no longer felt the need to jump to the defense. Most important, I no longer felt condemned. Instead, I felt encouragement with every page

I turned. In the end, I kept the manuscript and read it over several times. Admittedly, there are still passages that make me stumble, but the message of hope remains dominant.

If reading this book makes you frustrated – like I was – take time to evaluate the source of your frustration. Allow yourself to re-read it and view its message from a hopeful perspective: how could this help or heal my hurt?

I'm warning you now, this is not a book you can make compromises with. If your goal is a strong Christian relationship or marriage, remember that if you're going to reach that goal, you can't stray off the path with either foot. The key is to try to understand this book with an open heart. I truly feel that it is changing my life. Perhaps it will do the same for you.

M.L.
October 1995

CONTENTS

FOREWORD

I n *A Plea for Purity* we find a message needed today in every part of the world. To be pure, to remain pure, can only come at a price, the price of knowing God and of loving him enough to do his will. He will always give us the strength we need to keep purity as something beautiful for God. Purity is the fruit of prayer. If the family prays together they will remain in unity and purity, and love each other as God loves each one of them. A pure heart is the carrier of God's love, and where there is love, there is unity, joy, and peace.

Mother Teresa of Calcutta
November 1995

INTRODUCTION

E verywhere today, people are searching for lasting
and meaningful relationships. The myth of romance
continues to be taken for granted by millions, and a
new generation of young men and women has accepted
the belief that sexual freedom is the key to fulfillment.
But as desperately as people want to believe in the sexual
revolution of the last few decades, it is clear to many of
them that something has gone terribly wrong. Instead of
bringing freedom, it has left countless wounded and isolated souls. As we face the great anguish around us, it is
more important than ever for all of us, young and old,
to consider the direction of our lives and ask ourselves
where we are headed.

The twenty-first century heralds the loss of the clear
teachings of the Old and New Testaments on marriage
and the relationship of the sexes. We have turned against
God and rebelled against his order of creation, and we
have justified our rebellion with human arguments. We
have ignored the words of Jesus and scorned the voice
of the Spirit. But we have found neither freedom nor
fulfillment.

As a pastor I have counseled many people over the
years, both single and married. For so many of them, the

sexual sphere is not an area of joy but one of frustration, confusion, and even despair. People look for unity of heart and soul with one another, but they are so blinded by the notion of romantic love that their deepest longings remain obscured. They know that marriage and sexual union is a gift from God; that it should be the most intimate and rewarding relationship a man and a woman can share. But they wonder why it has become the source of such loneliness and pain for them and for so many others.

Again and again I have seen that when people are willing to surrender their lives to Jesus, they are able to find a way out of their unhappiness. Again and again I have seen that once people have the courage and humility to face his call to repentance, he can bring them genuine freedom and happiness.

Jesus brings true revolution. He is the original source of love, because he is Love itself. His teaching is neither a matter of prudishness nor of permissiveness: he offers his followers an entirely different way. He brings a purity that liberates us from our sin and leads to the possibility of a completely new life.

There is very little in today's culture that nurtures or protects the new life that Jesus wants to give us. People talk incessantly about the importance of committed marriages and wholesome family life, but how many of us are willing to take action to make these values a concrete reality? Many of us are tempted to blame society for the influences that corrupt us. But what about us so-called

Christians? How many of us are ready to unplug the television set and take a hard look at our own marriages and relationships and our personal lives? How many of us actually support the brothers and sisters around us in the daily struggle for purity? How many of us stick out our necks to confront the sin in each other's lives? How many of us are really accountable?

There is tremendous pain among those who claim to be followers of Christ: broken families, battered wives, neglected and abused children, and sinful relationships. Yet instead of an outcry, there is indifference. When will we wake up and realize that our apathy is destroying us?

More than ever, we need to come back to an understanding of the church as a living body of committed members who share life in practical deeds of love. But we must start with ourselves first and then see where we can encourage those around us. We need to know our youth well enough to be able to guide them as they seek relationships and lifetime commitments; we need to provide ongoing support for the marriages around us; we need to work for healing when our brothers or sisters stumble or fall – and accept their help when we ourselves have fallen.

Most of all, we must show the world that the unique teachings of Jesus and his apostles are the only answer to the spirit of our time. That is why I have put together this little book. I do not consider myself a writer or a biblical scholar. I am also fully aware that most of what I have written is completely contrary to popular wisdom. But I do feel the urgent need to share my certainty that Jesus' call to a life of love, purity, honesty, and commitment is our only hope.

This is not only a personal book – it comes out of the life of the Bruderhof, the church community to which I belong, and everything I have written is an attempt to express the united feeling of our members. Our concern and longing is that all of us – all men and women of our time – might stop to reconsider God's purpose for sex and marriage.

Many people today have simply given up on the possibility of a pure life. They have bought into the myth of sexual "liberation" and tried to live with its disappointments, and when their relationships fall apart, they explain away their failures. They fail to see what a tremendous gift purity is.

All the same, we believe that deep in every heart there is a yearning for unclouded relationships and for a love that lasts. It takes courage and self-discipline to really *live* a different way, but it is possible. Wherever there is a faithful church – a community of people who are committed to living in genuine and honest relationships – there is help and hope for every person and every marriage. May this book give each reader that faith.

J. C. A.
November 1995

IN THE BEGINNING

CHAPTER 1

IN THE IMAGE OF GOD

God said, "Let us make man in our image and likeness to rule the fish in the sea, the birds of heaven, the cattle, all wild animals on earth, and all reptiles that crawl upon the earth." So God created man in his own image; in the image of God he created him, male and female. God blessed them and said to them, "Be fruitful and increase; till the earth and subdue it" (Gen. 1:26–28).

I n the opening chapter of the story of creation we read that God created humankind – both male and female – in his own image, and that he blessed them and commanded them to be fruitful and to care for the earth. Right from the start, God shows himself as the creator who "saw all that he had made, and it was very good." Here, right at the beginning of the Bible, God reveals his heart to us. Here we discover God's plan for our lives.

Many, if not most, twentieth-century Christians dismiss the story of creation as a myth. Others insist that only the strictest, most literal interpretation of Genesis is valid. I simply have reverence for the word of the Bible as it stands. On the one hand, I would not think of arguing away anything in it; on the other, I believe scientists are

right in cautioning that the Bible should not be taken
too literally. As Peter says, "With the Lord, a day is like
a thousand years, and a thousand years like one day"
(2 Pet. 3:8).

GOD'S IMAGE SETS US APART

Exactly how human beings were created remains a mystery for the creator alone to unveil. Yet I am sure of one
thing: no person can find meaning or purpose without
God. Rather than dismiss the creation story simply because we do not understand it, we need to find its inner,
true meaning and rediscover its significance for us today.

In our depraved age, the reverence for God's plan as
described in Genesis has been almost completely lost.
We do not treasure the meaning of creation enough – the
significance of both man and woman as creatures formed
in the image and likeness of God. This likeness sets
us apart in a special way from the rest of creation and
makes each human life sacred (Gen. 9:6). To view life in
any other way – for instance, to view others only in the
light of their usefulness, and not as God sees them – is
to disregard their worth and dignity.

What does creation "in God's image" mean? It means
that we are to be a living picture of who God is. It means
that we are to be co-workers who further his work of
creating and nurturing life. It means that we belong to
him, and that our being, our very existence, should always remain related to him and bound to his authority.

The moment we separate ourselves from God we lose sight of our purpose here on earth.

In Genesis we read that we have the living spirit of God: "The Lord God formed man from the dust of the ground and breathed into his nostrils the breath of life, and man became a living being" (Gen. 2:7). In giving us his spirit, God made us responsible beings who possess the freedom to think and act, and to do so in love.

But even if we possess a living spirit, we remain only images of the creator. And when we look at creation in a God-centered, not human-centered, way we will understand our true place in his divine order of things. The person who denies that God is his origin, who denies that God is a living reality in his life, will soon be lost in a terrible emptiness. Ultimately, he will find himself trapped in the self-idolatry that brings with it self-contempt and a contempt for the worth of others.

ALL OF US LONG FOR WHAT IS IMPERISHABLE

What would we be if God had not breathed his breath into us? Darwin's whole theory of evolution, by itself, is dangerous and futile because it is not God-centered. Something inside each of us cries out against the idea that we have been hatched by a purposeless universe. Deep within the human spirit is a thirst for what is lasting and imperishable.

Since we are made in God's image, and God is eternal, we cannot, at the end of life, merely vanish again like

smoke. Our life is rooted in eternity. Christoph Blumhardt* writes, "Our lives bear the mark of eternity,
of the eternal God who created us to be his image.
He does not want us to be swallowed up in the transi-
tory, but calls us to himself, to what is eternal."[1]

God has set eternity in our hearts, and deep within
each of us is a longing for eternity. When we deny this
and live only for the present, everything that happens to
us in life will remain cloaked in tormenting riddles, and
we will remain deeply dissatisfied. No person, no human
arrangement, can ever fill the longing of our souls.

The voice of eternity speaks most directly to our conscience. Therefore the conscience is, perhaps, the deepest
element within us. It warns, rouses, and commands us
in our God-given task (Rom. 2:14–16). And every time
the soul is wounded, our conscience makes us painfully
aware of it. If we listen to our conscience, it can guide us.
When we are separated from God, however, our conscience will waver and go astray. This is true not only
for an individual, but also for a marriage.

Already in Genesis, chapter 2, we read about the importance of marriage. When God created Adam, he said
that everything he had made was good. Then he created
woman to be a helpmate and partner to man, because he
saw that it was not good for man to be alone. This is a
deep mystery: man and woman – the masculine and the
feminine – belong together as a picture of who God is,
and both can be found in him. Together they become
what neither would be apart and alone.

*Christoph Friedrich Blumhardt (1842–1919), German pastor, author,
and religious socialist.

Everything created by God gives us an insight into his
nature – mighty mountains, immense oceans, rivers and
great expanses of water; storms, thunder and lightning,
huge icebergs; meadows, flowers, trees, and ferns. There
is power, harshness, and manliness, but there is also
gentleness, motherliness, and sensitivity. And just as the
various forms of life in nature do not exist without each
other, God's children, too, male and female, do not exist
alone. They are different, but they are both made in
God's image, and they need each other to fulfill their true
destinies.

WHEN GOD'S IMAGE IS DEFACED, LIFE'S RELATIONSHIPS LOSE PURPOSE

It is a tragedy that in much of today's society the differences between man and woman are blurred and
distorted. The pure, natural image of God is being destroyed. There is endless talk about women's equality,
but in practice women are abused and exploited more
than ever before. In films, on television, in magazines,
and on billboards the ideal woman (and increasingly,
the ideal man) is portrayed as a mere sex object.

Generally speaking, marriages in our society are no
longer regarded as sacred. Increasingly they are seen as
experiments or as contracts between two people who
measure everything in terms of their own interests. When
marriages fail, there is almost always the option of no-
fault divorce, and after that a new attempt at marriage
with a new partner. Many people no longer even bother

to make promises of faithfulness; they just live together.
Women who bear and raise children or stay married to
the same husband are sometimes scorned. And even
when their marriage is a healthy one, they are often seen
as victims of oppression who need to be "rescued" from
male domination.

Children are often no longer treasured. In Genesis,
God commanded, "Be fruitful and increase." Today we
avoid the "burden" of unwanted offspring by means of
legalized abortion. Children are viewed as a bother; they
are too expensive to be brought into the world, to be
raised, to be given a college education. They are an economic strain on our materialistic lives. They are even too
time-consuming to love.

Is it any wonder that so many in our time have lost
hope? That so many have given up on the possibility
of enduring love? Life has lost its value; it has become
cheap; most people no longer see it as a gift from God.
But without God, life is like death, and there is only darkness and the deep wound of separation from him.

Despite the efforts of many dedicated individuals, the
church today has failed miserably in grappling with this
situation. All the more, each of us must go back to the
beginning and ask ourselves once again, "Why did God
create man and woman in the first place?" God created
every person in his image, and he has set a specific task
for every man, woman, and child on this earth, a task he
expects us to fulfill. No one can disregard God's purpose

for his creation or for himself without suffering deep inner need (Psa. 7:14–16).

The materialism of our time has emptied life of moral and spiritual purpose. It hinders us from seeing the world with awe and wonder, and it hinders us from seeing our true task. The sickness of soul and spirit brought about by consumerism has eaten so deeply into our conscience that it is no longer able to mirror good and evil clearly. Yet there is still a deep-seated need in each of us that makes us long for goodness.

We will find healing only if we believe firmly that God created us and that he is the giver of life, love, and mercy. As we read in the third chapter of the Gospel of John, "God so loved the world that he gave his only son, that whoever believes in him should not perish but have eternal life. For God sent his son into the world, not to condemn the world, but that the world might be saved through him."

In God's son – in Jesus – the creator's image appears with utmost clarity and finality (Col. 1:15). As the perfect image of God, and as the only way to the Father, he brings us life and unity, joy and fulfillment. Only when our life is lived in him can we experience his truth and goodness, and only in him can we find our true destiny. This destiny is to be God's image; to rule over the earth in his spirit, which is the creative, life-giving spirit of love.

CHAPTER 2

IT IS NOT GOOD FOR MAN TO BE ALONE

Then the Lord God said, "It is not good for the man to be alone. I will provide a partner for him..." So the Lord God caused the man to fall into a deep sleep; and while he was sleeping, he took one of the man's ribs and closed up the place with flesh. Then the Lord God made a woman from the rib he had taken out of the man, and he brought her to the man. Then the man said, "Now this at last is bone of my bones and flesh of my flesh; she shall be called 'woman,' for she was taken out of man" (Gen. 2:18, 21–23).

There is little that is so difficult for a person to bear as loneliness. Prisoners held in solitary confinement have told of rejoicing to see even a spider – at least it is *something* alive. God created us to be communal beings. Yet our modern world is frighteningly uncommunal. In many areas of life, technological progress has resulted in the deterioration of community. Increasingly, machines have made people seem unnecessary.

As the elderly are placed into retirement communities or personal-care homes, as factory workers are replaced by hi-tech machinery, as young men and women search year after year for meaningful work, they fall into despair and hopelessness. Some depend on the help of therapists or psychologists, and others seek avenues of escape such as alcoholism, drugs, and suicide. Cut off from God and each other, thousands of people lead lives of quiet desperation.

GOD CREATED US TO LIVE
WITH AND FOR OTHERS

God has planted in each of us an instinctive longing to achieve a closer likeness to him, a longing that urges us toward love, community, and unity. In his last prayer, Jesus points out the importance of this longing: "May they all be one, as thou, Father, art in me, and I in thee, so also may they be in us, that the world may believe that thou didst send me" (Jn. 17:20–21).

To live in isolation from others kills this unity and leads to despair. Thomas Merton writes:

> Despair is the absolute extreme of self love. It is reached when a man deliberately turns his back on all help from anyone else in order to taste the rotten luxury of knowing himself to be lost...
>
> Despair is the ultimate development of a pride so great and so stiff-necked that it selects the absolute misery of damnation rather than accept happiness

from the hands of God and thereby acknowledge
that he is above us and that we are not capable
of fulfilling our destiny ourselves.

But a man who is truly humble cannot despair,
because in a humble man there is no longer any
such thing as self-pity.[2]

We see here that pride is a curse that leads to death.
Humility, however, leads to love. Love is the greatest gift
given to humankind; it is our true calling. It is the "yes"
to life, the "yes" to community. Love alone fulfills the
longing of our innermost being.

No one can truly live without love: it is God's will for
every person to be the "thou" for every other. Every person is called to love and help those around him on God's
behalf (Gen. 4:8–10).

God wants us to find community with one another
and to help one another in love. And there is no doubt
that when we meet our brother's or sister's inmost heart,
we can help them, for "our" help is given by God himself. As John says, "We know that we have passed out of
death into life, because we love our brethren. He who
does not love abides in death" (1 Jn. 3:14). Our lives are
fulfilled only when love is kindled, proved, and brought
to fruition.

Jesus tells us that the two most important commandments are to love God with our whole heart, soul, and
strength, and to love our neighbor as ourselves. And
these two commandments cannot be separated: love to
God must always mean love to one's neighbor. We can-

not find a relationship to God if we disregard others
(1 Jn. 4:19–21). Our way to God must be through our
brothers and sisters, and in marriage, through our partner.

If we are filled with God's love, we can never be
lonely or withdrawn for long; we will always find someone to love. God and our neighbor will always be near
us. All we need to do is find them. When we suffer
from loneliness, it is often simply because we desire to
be loved rather than to give love. Real happiness comes
from giving love to others. We need to seek community
of love with our neighbor again and again, and in this
seeking we must each become a helper, a brother or a
sister. Let us ask God to free our choked-up hearts for
this love, knowing that we can find it only in the humility
of the cross.

EVERY PERSON CAN BE
AN INSTRUMENT OF GOD'S LOVE

In the story of the creation of Adam and Eve it is clear
that man and woman were created to help, to support, to
complement each other. What a joy it must have been for
God to bring woman to man – and man to woman! Because we are all made in the image of God, in his likeness, we must all find each other in joy and love, whether
we are married or not.

By bringing Eve to Adam, God shows all humans their
true calling – to be helpers who reveal his love to the
world. And by bringing us his son, Jesus, he shows us
that he will never leave us lonely or without help. Jesus

himself said, "I will not leave you orphaned; I will come
to you." He promises us that "the one who has received
my commandments and obeys them – he it is who loves
me; and he who loves me will be loved by my Father; and
I will love him and disclose myself to him" (Jn. 14:18–21).

Who can understand the depth of these words and the
hope they bring to our troubled world? The loneliest,
most discouraged, disillusioned people, even if they are
unable to find any human friendship, may be assured that
they are never alone. If they do not forsake God, they
will never be forsaken by him.

God brought Adam and Eve together to heal their loneliness and to set them free from their onesidedness, and
he has the same plan for every man and woman he brings
together in marriage. Yet marriage in itself cannot bring
wholeness. Unless we abide in Christ, we will bear no
fruit. When we love him who alone is our support, our
hope, and our life, we can be secure in knowing and
loving one another. But if we isolate ourselves inwardly
from Christ, nothing will go well. He alone holds everything together and gives us access to God and to others
(Col. 1:17–20).

GOD IS THE SOURCE
AND THE OBJECT OF TRUE LOVE

Marriage is not the highest goal of life. God's image is
reflected most brightly and completely where there is love
first for him and then for our brothers and sisters. In a true
Christian marriage, then, the husband will lead his wife

and children not to himself, but to God. In the same way, a wife will support her husband as a helper, and together they will lead their children to honor them as father and mother, and to love God as their creator.

To be a helper to another on God's behalf is not just an obligation, but a gift. How different our relationships would be if we rediscovered this! We live in a time when fear and mistrust grip us everywhere we go. Where is love, the love that builds community and the church?

There are two kinds of love. One is turned selflessly toward others and their well-being. The other is possessive and limited to the ego. Augustine says,"Love is the self of the soul, the hand of the soul. When it holds one thing, it cannot hold something else. If it is to hold what one gives it, it has to put down what it is holding."[3] God's love desires nothing. It gives and sacrifices itself, for this is its joy.

Love always has its roots in God. May God give it that the power of his love grips us anew. It will lead us to others, to share our lives with them. More than that, it will lead us to the kingdom. Love is the secret of God's coming kingdom.

CHAPTER 3

THEY SHALL BECOME ONE FLESH

For this reason a man will leave his father and mother and be united to his wife, and they will become one flesh (Gen. 2:24).

Marriage is sacred. In the Old Testament, the prophets use it to describe God's relationship with his people Israel: "I will betroth you to me forever; I will betroth you in righteousness and justice, in love and compassion. I will betroth you in faithfulness, and you will acknowledge the Lord" (Hos. 2:19). God reveals his love to all people in a special way in the unique bond between husband and wife.

MARRIAGE IS MORE THAN LIVING HAPPILY TOGETHER

In the New Testament, marriage is used as a symbol for the unity of Christ with his church. In the Gospel of John, Jesus is compared to a bridegroom, and in Revelation we read that "the wedding of the Lamb has come, and his bride has made herself ready" (Rev. 19:7–9).

It is not without significance that Jesus changed water
into wine at a wedding; clearly, he had great joy in marriage. Yet it is equally clear that to Jesus, marriage is a
holy matter. He takes it so seriously that he speaks with
uncompromising sharpness against even the slightest step
toward its destruction: "Therefore what God has joined
together, let no one separate" (Mt. 19:6–9).

We can see from Jesus' sharpness what a horror
adultery is in the eyes of God. The whole Bible protests
against it, from the books of the Prophets, where the
idol worship of the children of Israel is called adultery
(Jer. 13:25–27), to Revelation, where we read of God's
wrath against the harlot. When the bond of marriage
is broken, love – the unity of spirit and soul between
two – is broken and smashed, and not only between the
adulterer and his spouse, but between himself and God.

In our present-day culture, the institution of marriage
is teetering on the brink of disaster. Much of what is
called love is nothing but selfish desire. Even in marriage
many couples live together selfishly. People are deceived
in thinking that fulfillment can be found without sacrifice
and faithfulness, and even though they may live together,
they are afraid to love each other unconditionally.

Still, amid millions of floundering and ruined marriages, God's love stands eternal and cries out for con
stancy and devotion. There is a voice deep within each
of us, however muffled, that calls us back to faithfulness.
On some level, all of us yearn to be united – with free

and open hearts – to "somebody"; to some other "thou."
And if we turn to God in the trust that such unity with
another is possible, we can find the fulfillment of our
longing.

True fulfillment comes from giving love to another person. Yet love does not only seek to give; it also longs to
unite. If I really love another person, I will be interested
in knowing what is in him and willing to be led out of
my onesidedness. In love and humility I will help him
to the possibility of a full awakening, first toward God,
and then toward others. True love is never possessive.
It always leads to the freedom of faithfulness and purity.

The faithfulness between a husband and wife is a reflection of God's eternal faithfulness, for it is God who
brings every true bond together. In God's faithfulness we
find the strength to let love flow through our lives, and to
let our gifts unfold for each other. In the love and unity
of the church it is possible to become of one spirit with
every brother and sister, and also to become of one heart
and soul with them (Acts 4:32).

SEXUAL LOVE CAN GIVE GOD'S LOVE VISIBLE FORM

There is a difference between the love of an engaged or
married couple and the love among brothers and sisters.
Nowhere is a person more dependent on another than in
marriage. There is a special joy in the heart of a married
person when the beloved is near; and even when separated, there is a unique bond between them. Through
the intimate relationship of marriage, something takes

place which may even show in a couple's faces. As von Gagern* says, "Often it is only through his wife that the husband becomes truly a man; and through her husband that the wife gains true womanhood."[4]

In a true marriage, each partner seeks the fulfillment of the other. By complementing each other, the union between husband and wife is enhanced. In their love for one another, through their faithfulness to one another, and in their fruitfulness, husband and wife reflect God's image in a mysterious and wonderful way.

In the unique bond of marriage we discover the deeper meaning of becoming one flesh. Obviously to become one flesh means to become one physically and sexually, but it is far more than that! It is a symbol of two people bound and melted together, heart, body, and soul, in mutual giving and total oneness.

When two people become one flesh, they are no longer two, but actually one. Their union is the fruit of more than companionship or partnership; it is the deepest intimacy. As Friedrich Nietzsche writes, it is brought about by "the resolve of two to create a unity which is more than those who created it. It is reverence for one another and for the fulfillment of such a resolve."[5]

Only in this reverence and oneness does marriage fulfill the demands of the sexual conscience. Through the will to have children, to be fruitful and to multiply, and through the togetherness that reflects the unity of God with his creation and his people, marriage gives visible form to God's outpouring love.

---

*Friedrich E. F. von Gagern (1914–), German Catholic psychiatrist. See Works Cited.

WHEN GOD IS AT THE CENTER OF
A MARRIAGE, FULL UNITY OF HEART,
SOUL, AND BODY IS POSSIBLE

In God's order of marriage there are at least three different levels of experience. The first, most wonderful level
is unity of spirit: the oneness of heart and soul in God.
In this oneness we can have community not only with
our spouse but with all believing persons. The second
level is unity of emotion: the current of love from one
heart toward another that is so strong that a person can,
so to speak, hear the heartbeat of another. The third level
is physical unity: the expression of oneness found when
two bodies are fused in perfect union.

Too many couples today are content with the third
level alone, or perhaps the second. A marriage based
only on the physical and emotional is doomed to disappointment. Even though waves of emotional or physical
attraction are natural, they can leave deep wounds if they
are not placed under Christ. The healthiest marriages are
those founded in the order of God – on unity of spirit,
heart, and soul.

Most people today, including those of us who claim to
be Christians, have no idea how much God has prepared
for those who truly love and honor him. The experiences
of the heart that God can give in a true engagement or
marriage are greater than we can imagine. Too many of
us live only in the world of the senses – of sleeping, eat-
ing, and drinking – and never take time to really turn to
what is much more vital: our inner life. This is also true

in so many marriages today. Sex is the focal point, and often unity of heart is not even sought for or mentioned. Is it any wonder that so few couples remain faithful to each other for life?

Anyone who has lived near the ocean knows something of nature's power in the pull of high and low tides. In marriage, as in friendship, there are high and low tides. When a relationship is at low ebb, it is all too easy for us to lose patience, to distance ourselves from our partner, and even to abandon efforts toward a renewal of love. When God is at the center, we can turn to him and find faith and strength even at our lowest ebb.

The more we live up to the image of God in which we are created, the more strongly will we sense that God must remain our center, and that his commandments are fitting for us. We will sense that his commandments are not laid on us as alien laws and commands. Rather, we will see that they are in keeping with our true nature as created in his image. But the more we betray and destroy God's image within us, the more his rulership will appear to us as something foreign, a moral compulsion that crushes us.

To be fruitful for each other, by complementing each other in love, and to be fruitful with each other in bearing children – it is these purposes that make marriage blessed and holy, and a joy in heaven. Even so, in the story of the creation, before God's command "to be fruitful," comes a blessing: his gift of a partner to the first man. In giving the man this gift, it is as if God is saying, "My image lives in you." Whenever we approach marriage, we must consider this with great reverence. In every person and in every marriage lives the potential for a genuine expression of the image of God.[6]

CHAPTER 4

THE FIRST SIN

Now the serpent was more crafty than any of the wild animals
the Lord God had made. He said to the woman, "Did God really
forbid you to eat from any tree in the garden?" "You will not
surely die," the serpent said to the woman. "For God knows that
when you eat of it your eyes will be opened, and you will be like
God, knowing good and evil" (Gen. 3:1,4–5).

When God created the world, he saw that
everything he made was good. The earth
was truly his kingdom, and life was ruled
by the spirit of peace. Everything, including man and
woman, dwelled together in unity and harmony and took
delight in one another and in all that God had made. With
trembling reverence and wonder Adam and Eve stood
before the life-filled tree in the Garden of Eden. But then
the serpent misled Adam and Eve. Immediately, evil came
into God's creation and tried to destroy it completely.

Eve was tempted by the serpent with one simple question: "Did God really say that?" and with one simple promise: "Surely you will not die!" It is important that we
understand what this means. Satan, the seducer, tempted
Eve with words of God, just as later he tempted Jesus with
words of God.

PRIDE SEPARATES US FROM GOD
AND FROM EACH OTHER

What else was it, if not pride, when Eve looked at the
tree and lusted for its fruit, wanting to make herself like
God? Was she not testing God to see whether he would
really keep his word? The serpent put doubt into her
heart, and Eve listened to him with great curiosity. That in
itself was a betrayal of God, and it gives us an insight into
how Satan still works today.

Satan still wants to separate us from God, from our
brothers and sisters, and from our neighbor. And if we
are not watchful, he can do it simply by asking a seemingly innocent question that sows seeds of mistrust and
division in our hearts. Satan disguises himself as an angel
of light (2 Cor. 11:14), but actually he is the slanderer, the
twister of truth, the father of lies, the murderer from the
beginning; he tries to throw us into disorder and confusion and doubt – and very often he succeeds.

In the Gospel of Matthew we read that shortly after
Jesus' baptism, when he withdrew into the wilderness,
Satan tried to tempt him. Knowing that Jesus was physically weak after fasting for forty days, Satan approached
Jesus with a face of compassion and showed false reverence by suggesting that all the kingdoms of the world
should belong to him.

Yet already in that first temptation, Jesus recognized
Satan as the tempter, and the twister of truth. He trusted
in God unconditionally and did not consider listening to
Satan for even a moment, but rather went the way of

trust, obedience, and dependence on God. Satan could not
come close to his heart.

It was not just the forbidden fruit that enticed Adam
and Eve, but pride and the self-seeking desire to be like
God. Because they lacked trust, obedience, and dependence, they cut themselves off from God. In the end,
because they no longer honored him, they made idols
of each other.

The greatest curse on our human destiny is the attempt
to become like God. Bonhoeffer says, "In following Satan's
temptations to be like God yet independent of him, man
has become a god against God."[7] The result is a deep sickness in the human spirit. The image of God is now a sto-
len image, and twisted by idolatry and rebellion against
him, it brings great darkness and need (Rom. 1:23–32).

FALSE LOVE HINDERS THE JOY OF TOTAL GIVING

Adam and Eve both sinned against love. They were deceived by a false love. How many things happen today
that go by the name of love and are nothing but destruction and soul-murder!

> True love wants the person of God to shine through
> the beloved: God remains the value by which love is
> measured and the final goal of love's striving. But
> man, in a false love to the beloved, turns away from
> the highest good and thereby makes it impossible for
> God to shine through the beloved.[8]

All this should be a serious warning to us, whether we are

married or hoping to be married. God alone must be first
in our lives, not our partner, not our children. Otherwise
we will eventually lose touch with God and with each
other. Like Adam, we will no longer see God's counte-
nance or truly love him; we will see only our partner's.
Our love will become false love. It will open the door
to many evils, especially in the sexual area, and lead to
inner deadness and isolation.

Adam and Eve lost their innocence because they lost
their unity with God. And through the terrible emptiness
that followed, man blamed woman and sought to dominate, and woman, resentful of man, blamed Satan. All
unity was destroyed, and man and woman became rivals
and were no longer one (Gen. 3:7–19).

When our marriages are separated from God, rivalry
soon takes root and selfishness rules us. In competing
with our partner to rule the roost, we strive to create our
own little paradise on our own terms, and we soon sink
into emptiness and deep discontent. Our inner bond is
destroyed and we remain bound to one another only
through infatuation. We continually blame each other
and seek our own advantage and independence. The
joy of total giving is gone and only the curse of half-
heartedness is left.

The enemy of life in God is an independent and covet-
ous will. As my grandfather Eberhard Arnold* writes,
this will is "the commercial spirit of mammon, the legal
spirit of property-based relationships, the detachment

---

*Eberhard Arnold (1883–1935); writer, theologian, and co-founder
(with his wife Emmy) of the Bruderhof. See p. 154 below.

of sexual desire from the soul and from unity and community of spirit...All this is death; it is no longer connected with life."[9]

Anything that stands in opposition to life and love is evil, and as Christians we should never underestimate the power of evil. Sin always leads to separation, and the wages of sin are always death (Rom. 6:23). Sinful pride bears its bitter fruit in estrangement, separation from God, from our true selves, from others, and from the earth. Satan and sin shatter the most fundamental relationships we have.

From ancient times on, Christians have pictured Satan as a creature with hooves and horns. Such a notion has no biblical basis. Satan and his demons surround the earth as a force of evil – like an atmosphere (Eph. 2:1–2; 6:12). His sole aim is to blind humans with self-interest and egoism: "You will be like God." And instead of going the way of simple obedience, we allow ourselves to be tempted.

LIKE ADAM AND EVE, ALL OF US ARE DIVIDED AND ESTRANGED BY OUR SIN

Adam and Eve's first sin symbolizes the fall of each one of us. We cannot ignore the fact that the original image of God in us has been terribly distorted. Instead of being content to reflect the image of God, we strive for equality with God. We have turned the highest qualities within us against God's will. In our worldly "freedom" we are no longer even concerned about God or his original image. We are estranged from him and moved only by the affairs of the world. We are at odds with ourselves and trapped by the guilt of our own dividedness.

Cut off from God in this way, we place ourselves at the center of the universe and try to find peace in materialism and pleasure. But these idols only leave us troubled with anxiety and anguish. Then arises the first mistrustful question, "Why?" and the second, "Is God really there?" We begin to doubt the guidance of the Spirit, and we ask, "Why do I have it so hard? Why me?"

Such questions eat away at our trust, and when we ask them we are never far from sinning. Complete trust takes the hand that God is offering and goes the way he leads. Even if the way leads through darkness or suffering, through hard places, over rocks and deserts, trust will help us to follow. If we take God's hand, nothing can happen to us. But as soon as we let go of God and question him, we will begin to despair. That is always the challenge: to hold on to God.

Jesus had to endure every human suffering; he was spared nothing – not hunger, thirst, loneliness, nor torment. But he did not attempt to escape from his misery. He is near to us, and he is always ready to help us, to give us the strength to overcome (Heb. 2:14–18). Even the most satanic temptations, the most terrible hours of darkness, are overcome by these words of Jesus: "You shall worship the Lord your God, and him alone shall you serve" (Mt. 4:10). This is the secret. Here Satan loses all power over us, and the first sin no longer binds.

CHAPTER 5

RESTORING THE IMAGE OF GOD

The Lord is the Spirit, and where the Spirit of the Lord is, there is freedom. And we, who with unveiled faces all reflect the Lord's glory, are being transformed into his likeness with ever-increasing glory, which comes from the Lord, who is the Spirit...Therefore, if anyone is in Christ, he is a new creation; the old has gone, the new has come! (2 Cor. 3:17–18; 5:17)

Stronger than any human relationship is our relationship to God. All other relationships are merely symbols of it. First and foremost, we are images of God and we need to find reverence for that fact again and again.

The greatest hope for every seeker, and for every relationship or marriage, is to recognize that even though we have distorted this image and fallen away from God, a faint reflection still remains in us. Despite our corruption, God does not want us to lose our destiny as creatures made in his image. Therefore he sent his son Jesus, the second Adam, to break into our hearts (Rom. 5:17–19). Through Jesus the image of God can be restored in every man and woman, and to every relationship.

JESUS OPENS THE WAY TO GOD
AND TO EACH OTHER

Jesus is God's reconciler: he has come to reconcile us to
God and to others and to overcome the inner discord in
our lives (Eph. 2:11–19). When we become discouraged or
downcast, then more than ever we must seek him. Everyone who seeks will find God. This is a promise. Jeremiah
says, "You will seek me and find me when you seek me
with all your heart" (Jer. 29:13). And there are the wonderful words in the gospels: "Anyone who seeks will find; to
anyone who knocks, the door will be opened" (Lk. 11:10).
These words are true today, and if we take them seriously,
God will become living in our hearts.

The way to God is open for everyone. No human being
is excluded from this gift, because Jesus came as a human
being. God sent him to restore his image in us. Through
him we have access to the Father. But this can only happen when the experience of Pentecost – the experience
of personal repentance, conversion, and faith – becomes
a burning reality for us.

The miracle of Pentecost, in which the Spirit descended
to earth in power and love, can happen anywhere in the
world at any time. It can happen wherever people cry out,
"Brothers, sisters, what shall we do?" and wherever they
are ready to hear the age-old answer of Peter, "Repent and
be baptized, every one of you, in the name of Jesus the
Messiah, for the forgiveness of your sins…Save yourselves
from this crooked generation" (Acts 2:37–40).

FREEDOM COMES THROUGH SURRENDER, NOT HUMAN STRENGTH

We can find forgiveness and salvation only at the cross. At the cross we undergo death. This death liberates us from everything that has prevented fellowship with God and with others and renews our relationship with them. In giving up the sin and evil which has enslaved us, we find freedom in Jesus. We can never redeem ourselves or better ourselves by our own strength. All we can finally do is surrender ourselves completely to Jesus and his love, so that our lives no longer belong to us but to him.

My father, J. Heinrich Arnold, writes:

> If we want to be healed of the wounds made by Satan's tricks and arrows...we must have the same absolute trust in Jesus as he had in God. Ultimately, all we have is our sin. But we must lay our sin before him in trust. Then he will give us forgiveness, cleansing, and peace of heart; and these lead to a love that cannot be described.[10]

What does it mean to "lay our sin before him in trust"? Freedom and the possibility for reconciliation begin whenever we confess the accusations of our conscience. Sin lives in darkness and wants to remain there. But when we bring to light the sins that burden us – when we admit them without reserve – we can be cleansed and freed. Ultimately, we have to stand before God. We cannot run away or hide from him, as Adam and Eve tried to do when they disobeyed him. If we are willing to stand

before him in the light of his son Jesus, he will burn away
all our guilt.

Just as God gave the first man and woman peace and
joy in the Garden of Eden, he gives every believer the task
of working toward the new order of his peaceable kingdom. To carry out this task, we must joyfully accept the
rule of God in our lives and be willing to go the entire way
of Jesus – to start at the stable in Bethlehem and end at the
cross on Golgotha. It is a very lowly, humble walk. But it
is the only way that leads to complete light and hope.

Jesus alone can forgive and remove our sins, because
he alone is free from all stain. He can stir our consciences
and set them free from impurity, bitterness, and discord
(Heb. 9:14). If we accept the stirring of the conscience,
if we embrace God's judgment and mercy, it does not matter how sinful and corrupt we have been. In Christ the
conscience that used to be our enemy becomes our friend.

FORGIVENESS HAS POWER
TO TRANSFORM OUR LIVES

The forgiveness of sins that Jesus offers is so powerful that
it will change a person's life completely. Everything that
makes us fearful or isolated, everything impure and deceit-
ful, will yield if we give ourselves to him. What is up will
come down, and what is down will come up. This change
will start in the innermost heart of our being, and then
both our inner and outer life, including all our relationships, will be transformed.

Whether or not a person has been transformed in this
way shows up most plainly when he or she faces death.
Those who have been at the bedside of a dying person
will know how absolute, how final in its significance,
is each person's inner relationship and bond with God.
They know that in the end, when the last breaths are
drawn, this bond is the only thing that counts.

It is the life-task of every person to prepare to meet
God. Jesus tells us how to do this when he says, "Whatever you do for the least of them you do to me." He also
says, "Blessed are the poor in spirit, for theirs is the kingdom of God." I have personally experienced at deathbeds
that if a person has lived for others, as Jesus did, then
God is very close to him in the last hour. I have also experienced at the hour of death the torment of those who
have lived selfish and sinful lives.

All of us, married and single, need to grasp more
deeply the eternal, healing words of Jesus: "Lo, I am with
you always, even to the close of the age" (Mt. 28:20). In
Jesus there is life, love, and light. In him our lives and our
relationships can be purified from all that burdens us and
opposes love, and God's image in us can be restored.

CHAPTER 6

SEXUALITY AND THE SENSUOUS SPHERE

Everything God created is good, and nothing is to be rejected if it is received with thanksgiving, because it is consecrated by the Word of God and prayer (1 Tim. 4:4–5).

The Bible speaks of the heart as the center of a person's inner life. In the heart, decisions are made and the direction is set as to what spirit we will follow (Jer. 17:10). But God also created us as sensuous beings. To the sensuous belongs everything that we perceive with our senses, including sexual attraction. The scent of a flower, the warmth of the sun, or a baby's first smile brings us joy. God has given us a great gift in our senses, and if we use them to praise and honor him, they can bring us great happiness.

Yet just as the area of sensuous experience can bring us close to God, it can mislead us and even bring us into satanic darkness. All too often we tend toward the superficial and miss the might and power of what God could

*For chapters 6 and 7, the author acknowledges his indebtedness to Catholic philosopher Dietrich von Hildebrand (1889–1977), especially his book *Purity: The Mystery of Christian Sexuality*. See Works Cited.

otherwise give us. Too often, in grasping at what we experience with our senses, we forget about God and miss the possibility of experiencing the full depth of his will.

LASTING JOY IS FOUND NOT IN OUR SENSES, BUT IN GOD

To reject the living senses is to reject God and his handiwork (1 Tim. 4:1–3). The Spirit does not want us to reject the body or its emotional powers. But we should not forget that Satan seeks to undermine every good thing; he is a twister of the truth and is always waiting to deceive us, especially in this area.

Admittedly, the soul is drawn to God through the spirit, but it is always bound to the physical through the body. The physical is not the real enemy of the spirit, and it must never be despised. The real enemy is Satan, who continually tries to attack the human soul and sever it from God. God's will is that every part of life – spirit, soul, and body – be brought under his control for his service (1 Cor. 10:31).

In and of itself there is nothing wrong with the sphere of the senses. After all, everything we do, whether waking or sleeping, is a sensory experience at some level. But because we are not mere animals, because we are made in the image of God, far more is expected of us.

When two people fall in love, the joy they have at first is on a sensuous level: they look into each other's eyes, they hear one another speak, they rejoice in the touch of the other's hand, or even in the warmth of the

other's closeness. Of course, the experience goes far
deeper than seeing, hearing, or feeling, but it still begins
as an experience of the senses.

Yet human love can never remain at this level – it must
go much deeper than that. When the sensuous becomes
an end in itself, everything seems fleeting and temporary,
and we feel compelled to seek our satisfaction in experiences of greater and greater intensity (Eph. 4:17–19).
Spending our energies in the intoxication of our senses,
we soon exhaust and ruin our ability to take in life's
vital power. And we also lose the capacity for any deep
inner experiences.

Unless we surrender ourselves (including our senses)
in reverence to God, we will be unable to experience the
things of this world to their fullest. In God we can experience the eternal in the sensuous. In him we can satisfy our
heart's deepest longings for what is genuine and lasting.

WHEN SURRENDERED TO GOD,
OUR SEXUALITY IS A GIFT

As a gift from God, sensuality is a mystery; without God,
its mystery is lost and it is desecrated. This is especially
true for the whole area of sex. The sexual life has a deep
intimacy all its own, which each of us instinctively hides
from others. Sex is each person's secret, something that
affects and expresses one's innermost being. Every disclo-
sure in this area opens up something intimate and personal and lets another person into one's secret. Therefore
the sexual sphere – even though it is one of God's greatest

gifts – is also the sphere of shame. We are ashamed to unveil our secret before others. There is a reason for this: just as Adam and Eve were ashamed of their nakedness before God because they knew that they had sinned, all of us know that we are sinful by nature. This recognition is not an unhealthy mental disorder, as modern psychologists claim. It is the instinctive response to protect that which is holy and given by God, and it should lead every person to repentance.

Sexual union is meant to be the expression and fulfillment of an enduring and unbreakable bond of love. It represents the supreme surrender to another human being because it involves the mutual revelation of each partner's most intimate secret. To engage in sexual activity of any kind without being united in the bond of marriage, therefore, is a desecration. The widespread practice of premarital sexual "experimentation," even with a partner one intends to marry, is no less terrible, and it can severely damage a future marriage. The veil of intimacy between a man and woman must not be lifted without the blessing of God and the church in marriage (Heb. 13:4).

Even within a marriage, the whole sphere of sexual intimacy must be placed under Christ if it is to bear good fruit. The contrast between a marriage where Christ is in the center and one where the flesh is the focal point is best described by the Apostle Paul in his letter to the Galatians:

> The acts of the sinful nature are obvious: sexual immorality, impurity, and debauchery; idolatry and

witchcraft; hatred, discord, jealousy, fits of rage, selfish ambition, dissensions, factions, and envy; drunkenness, orgies, and the like. I warn you, as I did before, that those who live like this will not inherit the kingdom of God. But the fruit of the Spirit is love, joy, peace, patience, kindness, goodness, faithfulness, gentleness, and self-control. Against such things there is no law. Those who belong to Christ Jesus have crucified the sinful nature with its passions and desires (Gal. 5:19–24).

People who see sexual lust in the same way as they see gluttony do not understand the significance of the sexual sphere. When we surrender to the temptations of lust or sexual impurity, we are defiled in quite a different way than by gluttony, even though that, too, is condemned by Paul. Lust and impurity wound us in our innermost heart and being. They attack the soul at its core. Whenever we fall into sexual impurity, we fall prey to demonic evil, and our whole being is corrupted. Then only through deep repentance and conversion can we be freed.

THE OPPOSITE OF IMPURITY IS NOT LEGALISM

The opposite of sexual impurity and sensuality, however, is not prudery, moralism, or false piety. How seriously Jesus warns us against this! (Mt. 23:25–28) In everything we experience with our senses, our joy must be genuine and free. Pascal says, "The passions are most alive in those who want to renounce them." When sensuality is repressed by moral compulsion rather than disciplined from within, it will only find new channels of untruthfulness and perversity (Col. 2:21–23).

In our corrupt and shameless time, it is harder and harder to raise children with a deep sense of reverence for God and all that he has created. All the more, we must strive to bring up our children in such a way that whether or not they marry as adults, they grow up to be men and women committed to a life of purity.

We must be watchful that our children do not talk irreverently about sexual matters. Yet at the same time, we cannot avoid the issue. Rather, we need to bring to our children a spirit of reverence. We must teach them to understand the significance and holiness of sex in God's order, and impress on them the importance of keeping their bodies pure and undefiled for the single purpose of marriage. They must learn to feel, as we do, that sex finds its greatest fulfillment, and therefore gives greatest pleasure, only in a pure and godly marriage.

God has joy when a young married couple experiences full uniting: first in spirit, then from heart to heart and soul to soul, and then in body. God has joy when a man and woman lift the veil of sex in reverence before him, in relationship with him, and in the unity given by him. Every couple should strive for this reverence, for "the pure in heart shall see God."

CHAPTER 7

THE PURE IN HEART

Blessed are the pure in heart, for they shall see God...Since we have these promises, dear friends, let us purify ourselves from everything that contaminates body and spirit, perfecting holiness out of reverence for God (Mt. 5:8; 2 Cor. 7:1).

Søren Kierkegaard says that purity of heart is to will one thing. That one thing is God and his will. Apart from God, our hearts remain hopelessly divided. What is impurity, then? Impurity is separation from God. In the sexual sphere it is the misuse of sex, which occurs whenever sex is used in any way that is forbidden by him.

Impurity never pollutes us from without. It cannot be outwardly wiped away at will. Originating in our imagination, it breaks out from inside us like an infected sore (Mt. 15:16–20). An impure spirit is never satisfied, never whole: it always wants to steal something for itself, and even then lusts for still more. Impurity stains the soul, corrupts the conscience, destroys the coherence of life, and eventually leads to spiritual death.

AN IMPURE HEART IS
NEITHER SATISFIED NOR FREE

Whenever we allow our soul to be touched by impurity, we open it to a demonic force that has power to gain control over every sphere of our life, not only the sexual. Impurity can take the form of idolatrous passion for professional sports; it can be the ambitious craving for prestige or power over other people. If we are ruled by anything but Christ, we are living in impurity.

Impurity in the sexual sphere consists in using another person solely in order to satisfy desire. It is there wherever people enter into situations of sexual intimacy with no intention of forming a lasting bond.

The starkest form of impurity occurs when a person engages in sexual intercourse (or any other sexual act) for the sake of money. A person who does this "becomes one with the harlot," as the Apostle Paul says, because he is using the body of another human being simply as a thing, a means of self-gratification. In doing this he commits a crime against the other person, but also against himself: "He who goes to the prostitute becomes the murderer of his own life" (1 Cor. 6:15–20). Even in marriage, sex for its own sake is sex separated from God. As von Hildebrand writes, it possesses a poisonous sweetness that paralyzes and destroys.

It would be a great mistake, however, to imagine that the opposite of impurity is the absence of sexual feeling. In fact, the lack of sexual awareness is not necessarily even fertile ground for purity. A person who lacks sensi-

tivity to sex is in actual fact an incomplete person: he or
she lacks something not only in natural disposition, but
in that which gives color to his or her whole being.

People who seek purity do not despise sex. They are
simply free from prudish fear and hypocritical shows of
disgust. But they never lose reverence for the mystery of
sex, and they will keep a respectful distance from it until
they are called by God to enter its territory through marriage.

God wants to give inner harmony and decisive clarity
to every heart. In this lies purity (Jas. 4:8). As Eberhard
Arnold writes:

> If one's heart is not clear and undivided – "single,"
> as Jesus put it – then it will be weak, flabby, and
> indolent, incapable of accepting God's will, of mak-
> ing important decisions, and of taking strong action.
> That is why Jesus attached the greatest significance
> to singleness of heart, simplicity, unity, solidarity,
> and decisiveness. Purity of heart is nothing else than
> absolute integrity, which can overcome desires that
> enervate and divide. Determined single-heartedness
> is what the heart needs in order to be receptive,
> truthful and upright, confident and brave, firm and
> strong.[11]

THE KEY TO PURITY IS HUMILITY

In the Beatitudes Jesus blesses the pure and the meek; he
says that they shall inherit the earth and see God. Purity
and meekness belong together, because they both arise

If you liked this book, you may want to:

- ☐ Order *A Plea for Purity* for a friend at $13.00* (£8.50) each.

- ☐ Order *Discipleship* (see p. 160) at $15.00 (£9.90) each.

- ☐ Receive information on the book about *Children's Education*, by the same author.

- ☐ Receive a free copy of our Plough Book Catalog.

- ☐ Receive a free sample copy of our magazine *The Plough*.

  Call about our discounts on quantity purchases.

NAME

ADDRESS

ADDRESS

TELEPHONE

To order, call us or fill in (on front of card) the address of the Plough office nearest to you.

In the USA

Spring Valley Bruderhof
Farmington, PA 15437
1-800-521-8011
412-329-1100

In the United Kingdom

Darvell Bruderhof
Robertsbridge, E. Sussex
TN32 5DR
0800-269-048
+44 (0) 1580-881-003

* Price valid through 12/96
Plough pays postage

The Plough Publishing House

from complete surrender to God. In fact, they depend on
it. But purity and meekness are not inborn; they must be
struggled for again and again. There are few things more
wonderful a Christian can strive for.

The struggle against sexual impurity is not just a prob-
lem for young adults. For many people, it does not lessen
as they grow older and more mature but remains a serious
struggle for life. Still, we can take courage. No matter how
often or how sorely we are tempted, Jesus will plead to
God on our behalf if we ask him. In him we will find victory over every temptation (1 Cor. 10:13).

Yet only the humble can experience God's infinite
goodness. The proud never can. Proud people open their
hearts to all sorts of evil: impurity, lying, stealing, and the
spirit of murder. Where there is one of these sins, the others will not be far behind. Self-confident people who strive
for purity in their own strength will always be stumbling.
Humble people, on the other hand, live in God's strength.
They may fall, but God will always lift them up.

Of course, not only our struggles but everything in our
lives should be placed under Jesus. Jesus overcomes the
desires that tear us apart and dissipate our strength. The
more firmly we are gripped by his Spirit, the nearer we
will come to finding our true character and true integrity.

WHO IS PURE IN HEART?

Bonhoeffer writes, "Who is pure in heart? Only those who
have surrendered their hearts completely to Jesus that he
alone may remain in them; only those whose hearts are

undefiled by their own evil – and by their own virtue
as well."[12]

In the Sermon on the Mount we can see how seriously
Jesus takes the daily fight for purity. He says that if we
look at another person with a lustful glance, we have
already committed adultery in our hearts (Mt. 5:27–30).
The fact that Jesus speaks about lustful thoughts – let
alone lustful actions – should show us how important a
decisive attitude of heart is in this fight.

Pure men and women are able to discern both the
good and the evil in the sexual sphere. They are awake
to its intrinsic qualities and fully aware of its goodness
and beauty as a gift from God. But they are also keenly
aware that even the slightest misuse of this gift opens the
door to evil spirits, and they know they cannot free themselves from these spirits in their own strength. That is
why they avoid every situation that defiles the soul and
abhor the thought of leading others into sin.

It is of vital importance that in our fight for purity we
reject everything that belongs to the domain of sexual
impurity, including greed, vanity, and every other form
of self-indulgence. Our attitude cannot be one of "partial"
fascination with lust – only one of complete rejection. If
our hearts are pure, we will react instinctively against
anything that threatens to cloud this attitude.

Here the church community has a great responsibility
to fight daily for an atmosphere of purity among all of its
members (Eph. 5:3–4). The fight for purity must go hand
in hand with the fight for justice and community, because

there is no true purity of heart without a feeling for justice (Jas. 1:26–27). Purity is not just related to the sexual
area; to know that a neighbor is hungry and to go to bed
without giving him food is to defile one's heart. That is
why the early Christians pooled everything they pos-
sessed – their food and drink, their goods, their strength,
even their intellectual and creative activity – and gave
them up to God. Because they were of one heart and
soul and held all things in common, they could fight all
things through to victory as one body.

MARRIAGE IS NO GUARANTEE OF PURITY

It is an illusion to think that the struggle for purity comes
to an end as soon as one is married. Marriage can even
be a trap. Many young people think that all their problems will be solved the minute they are married, but the
fact is that many of their problems will only begin then.

Certainly, the union between husband and wife is a
great grace. It has a redeeming effect, especially in the
sense of softening one's ego. But the redemptive effect
of marriage can never be complete in itself. No one can
ever solve the need of a partner's burdened conscience.
Full redemption can be found only in Jesus.

A marriage certificate is no guarantee of purity. Whenever a true relationship to God is missing, sex quickly
loses its true depth and dignity and becomes an end in
itself. Even in marriage, superficiality in the sexual sphere
spells ruin because it breaks down the mystery of the
bond between man and woman.

Nothing should reveal the need of God's special sanction more plainly than marriage. Therefore, whenever a
man and woman unite, they should have the attitude
Moses had when he came upon the burning bush: "Here
is holy ground, take off your shoes!" (Ex. 3:5) Their attitude must always be one of reverence for their creator
and for the mystery of marriage.

As the union of a husband and wife under God, sex
fulfills its divinely ordained function in a profound way:
it is tender, peaceful, and mysterious. Far from being an
animal-like act of aggression and lust, it creates and expresses a unique bond of deep, self-giving love.

When a couple experiences the sexual sphere in this
way, they will feel that their union cannot be meant only
for procreation. At the same time, they must remember
that through their uniting a new soul may be called out
of eternity to earth. If they are truly reverent, they will
feel such an awe for the holiness of this fact that their
union will become like a prayer to God.

Without Christ, a man or woman who has lived in
impurity cannot grasp the mysterious depth of the sexual
sphere. But in Christ there can be complete healing. "For
we know that when he appears, we shall be like him, for
we shall see him as he is. Everyone who has this hope in
him purifies himself, just as he is pure" (1 Jn. 3:3).

WHAT GOD HAS
JOINED TOGETHER

CHAPTER 8

MARRIAGE
IN THE HOLY SPIRIT

I urge you to live a life worthy of the calling you have received. Be completely humble and gentle; be patient, bearing with one another in love. Make every effort to keep the unity of the Spirit through the bond of peace (Eph. 4:1–3).

E very marriage goes through tests and crises, but these can bring about an increase in love, and every young couple should remember this. True love provides the strength needed to meet every test. It means deeds, acts of helping one another in humble, mutual submission. True love is born of the Holy Spirit.

THE SPIRIT OPENS UP AN ENTIRELY DIFFERENT PLANE OF EXPERIENCE

When two people seek a relationship, they usually do so in terms of mutual emotions, common values, shared ideas, and a feeling of good will toward each other. Without despising these, we must recognize that the Holy Spirit opens up an entirely different plane of experience between husband and wife.

Certainly, marital love based on the impulses of the emotions can be wonderful, but it can quickly become desperate and unhappy. In the long run it is an unstable foundation. Love gains certainty and firmness only when it is ruled by the Spirit.

If we seek only the unity and love that is possible on a human level, we remain like clouds drifting and suspended. When we seek unity in the Spirit, God can ignite in us a faithful love that can endure to the end. The Spirit burns away everything that cannot endure. He purifies our love. True love does not originate from ourselves, but is poured out over us.

Marriage in the Holy Spirit signifies faithfulness. Where there is no loyalty, there is no true love. In our society, marriages are being tested as never before, but this should refine and increase our faithfulness to one another. Faithfulness springs from the inward certainty of our calling. It comes from submission to God's order.

In his *Confession of Faith* (1540), the Anabaptist Peter Riedemann describes God's order for marriage as encompassing three levels. First is the marriage of God to his people, of Christ to his church, and of the Spirit to our spirit (1 Cor. 6:17). Second is the community of God's people among themselves – justice and common fellowship in spirit and soul. Third is the unity between one man and one woman (Eph. 5:31), which "is visible to and understandable by all."[13]

UNITY OF FAITH IS THE SUREST BASIS
FOR MARRIAGE

Paul the Apostle also draws a parallel between marriage
and spiritual unity when he tells husbands to love their
wives "just as Christ loved the church and gave himself
up for her" (Eph. 5:25). For Christians, marriage is a reflection of the deepest unity: the unity of God and his
church. In a Christian marriage, therefore, it is the unity
of God's kingdom, in Christ, and in the Holy Spirit that
matters most. Ultimately, it is the only sure foundation on
which a marriage can be built. "Seek first God's kingdom
and his justice, and all these things will be given to you
as well" (Mt. 6:33).

Marriage should always lead two believing people
closer to Jesus and his kingdom. But for this to take
place, they must first be fully dedicated as individuals to
the spirit of God's kingdom, and to the church community that serves it and stands under its direction. First
there must be unity of faith and spirit. Only then will
there be true unity of soul and body as well.

This is why, in our Bruderhof communities, we cannot
agree to the union of one of our members with a man or
woman who does not share our faith or the calling to live
in community with us (2 Cor. 6:14). (In Ezra, chapters 9
and 10, we read how he had to come before God and
repent deeply on behalf of all the Israelites because they
were marrying women from pagan nations.) On the one
hand, we believe that anyone who is really drawn by the

spirit of brotherliness and justice will not remain an
"outsider"; on the other, we feel that the marriage of one
of our members with a person who is not drawn to the
church and its search for full community would be un-
thinkable. It would contradict the unity of the Spirit that
is the highest level of marriage.

If, however, someone already married to a partner
holding a different belief wished to join our community,
we would do our utmost to save the marriage, as long as
the new member was not hindered in faith by the unbelieving partner.

When the love of two people who desire to be married is dedicated to the Holy Spirit and placed under his
rule and direction – when it serves the unity and justice
of God's kingdom – there is no reason why the two
should not marry. But when a couple lacks spiritual unity,
marriage in the church should be out of the question.
If the church is truly the Body, the unity of its members
under God must come before everything else.

Here it should be said that the demands of a true marriage in the Spirit can never be met by a human system
of answers or solved by means of principles, rules, and
regulations. They can be grasped only in the light of
unity, by those who have experienced the spirit of unity,
accepted it personally, and begun to live in accordance
with it.

The very essence of God's will is unity (Jn. 17:20–23).
It was God's will for unity that brought Pentecost to the

world. Through the outpouring of the Spirit, people's
hearts were struck, and they repented and were baptized.
The fruits of their unity were not only spiritual. The material and practical aspects of their lives, too, were affected
and even revolutionized. Goods were collected and sold,
and the proceeds were laid at the feet of the apostles.
Everyone wanted to give all they had out of love. Yet no
one suffered want, and everyone received what he or she
needed. Nothing was held back. There were no laws or
principles to govern this revolution. Not even Jesus said
exactly how it should be brought about, only, "Sell all
you have and give it to the poor" (Mt. 19:21). At Pentecost it simply happened: the Spirit descended and united
the hearts of those who believed (Acts 2:42–47).

THE SPIRIT FREES US FROM PETTINESS
AND BRINGS UNITY OF HEART

Genuine unity, like joy or love, cannot be forced or
created artificially. The Spirit alone can bring unity. The
Spirit alone can free us from our pettiness and from the
forces of guilt and sin that divide us from God and from
each other. With our own wills we can certainly try to
free ourselves from these forces, and we may be able to
overcome them to a certain degree and for a certain
period of time. But we should remember that ultimately
only the spirit of love can overcome the flesh.

Again, we must never forget our dependence on the
guidance of the Holy Spirit (Gal. 5:25). Even within a
marriage, if our unity is based only on mutual feelings

or common values and not on the Spirit, it runs the risk of being swallowed up by the purely sexual and emotional. We ourselves are not capable of bringing about the true unity of spirit in which two hearts become one. That can happen only when we allow ourselves to be gripped and transformed by something greater than ourselves.

When a marriage is anchored in the Holy Spirit, both partners will feel that their love is not a private possession but a fruit and gift of God's uniting love. They may still struggle with selfishness, disunity, superficiality, or other disorders, but if they keep their hearts open, the Spirit will always lift their eyes to God and his help.

The Spirit must come to each of us, whether married or unmarried, again and again. He wants to transform everything in our hearts and give us the strength to love. In his First Letter to the Corinthians, Paul says, "There is nothing love cannot face; there is no limit to its faith, its hope, and its endurance. Love will never come to an end." Love is born of the Holy Spirit, and only in the Spirit can a true marriage be conceived – and endure.

CHAPTER 9

THE MYSTERY OF MARRIAGE

Husbands, love your wives, just as Christ loved the church and gave himself up for her to make her holy, cleansing her by the washing with water through the Word, and to present her to himself as a radiant church, without stain or wrinkle or any other blemish, but holy and blameless. In this same way, husbands ought to love their wives as their own bodies. He who loves his wife loves himself. After all, no one ever hates his own body, but he feeds and cares for it, just as Christ does the church, for we are members of his body. For this reason a man will leave his father and mother and be united to his wife, and the two will become one flesh. This is a profound mystery, but I am talking about Christ and the church (Eph. 5:25 – 32).

In God's order, marriage and family originate in the church. The church is God's primary expression of his love and justice in the world. In the church, marriage can be fulfilled and given its true value. Without the church, it is doomed to be overcome by the dominating and destructive forces of society.

MARRIAGE IS MORE THAN A BOND
BETWEEN HUSBAND AND WIFE

Only very few people in our day understand that marriage contains a mystery far deeper than the bond of husband and wife, that is, the eternal unity of Christ with his
church. In a true marriage, the unity of husband and wife
will reflect this deeper unity. It is not only a bond between one man and one woman, because it is sealed by
the greater bond of unity with God and his people. This
bond must always come first. It is this bond we pledge
at baptism and reaffirm at every celebration of the Lord's
Supper, and we should remind ourselves of it at every
wedding. Without it, even the happiest marriage will bear
no lasting fruit.

How little the marriage bond amounts to when it is
only a promise or contract between two people! How
different the state of the modern family would be if Christians everywhere were willing to place loyalty to Christ
and his church above their marriages.

For those who have faith, Christ – the one who truly
unites – always stands between the lover and the beloved.
It is his Spirit that gives them unhindered access to one
another. Therefore, when sin enters a marriage and
clouds the truth of love, a faithful disciple will follow
Jesus in the church, not his or her wayward partner.

Emotional love will protest this because it is prone
to disregard the truth. It may even try to hinder the clear
light that comes from God. It is unable and unwilling to

dissolve a relationship, even when it becomes false and ungenuine. But true love never follows evil: it rejoices in the truth (1 Cor. 13:6).

Therefore, at each wedding in our community, a couple answers this decisive question: "If one of you should experience the shipwreck of your faith and leave the life of discipleship, will the other promise to put loyalty to Christ and the church above your marriage?" In other words, both partners must recognize that unity of faith is more important than the emotional bond of their marriage. This question is vital not only for Bruderhof couples, but for every man or woman anywhere who claims to be a disciple. If your first allegiance is not to Jesus and the church, who is it to? (Lk. 9:57–60)

When the smaller unity of a couple is placed under the greater unity of the church, their unity becomes steadfast and secure on a new, deeper level because it is placed within the unity of all believers. It is hardly surprising that this idea is foreign to most people. In today's culture, people think that the more independently a marriage is built, the firmer it is. Some even think that the more a couple can be relieved of the "constraints" of obligation to each other, the happier they will be. This is a completely false presumption. Only when a marriage is founded in God's order and on the basis of his love can it last. A marriage is built on sand unless it is built on the rock of faith.

MAN AND WOMAN HAVE DIFFERENT TASKS, AND THEY MUST COMPLEMENT EACH OTHER

The belief that love to Christ and his church must take priority over all else is also important for understanding the difference between man and woman. Clearly God has given each of them different natures and tasks, and when these are rightly fulfilled in a marriage in the church, harmony and love will abound. My father, J. Heinrich Arnold, writes:

> Obviously, there are differences in the biological makeup of the male and the female. But it is completely materialistic to think that the difference between man and woman is merely biological. A woman longs to absorb her beloved one into herself. She is designed by nature to receive and to endure; to conceive, to bear, to nurse, and to protect. A man, on the other hand, desires to enter his beloved one and become one with her; he is made to initiate and penetrate rather than to receive.[14]

It has been said that the body is shaped by the soul, and this is a deep thought. The soul, the breath of God, the innermost essence of each human being, forms a different body for each. It is never a question of who is higher. Both man and woman were made in the image of God, and what can be greater than that? Yet there is a difference: Paul likens man to Christ and woman to the

church (Eph. 5:22–24). Man, as Head, portrays the service of Christ. Woman, as Body, portrays the dedication
of the church. There is a difference in calling, but there
is no difference in worth.

Mary is a symbol of the church. In her we recognize
the true nature of womanhood and motherhood. Woman
is like the church because she receives and carries the
Word within her (Lk. 1:38) and brings life into the world
in keeping with God's will. This is the highest thing that
can be said of a human being.

A woman's way of love is different from that of a
man's. It is more steady, more in keeping with her loyal
nature. It is dedicated to protecting and guiding all those
in its care. Man's love, on the other hand, seeks others
out and challenges them. It is the pioneering love of the
apostle, of Christ's representative: "Go out and gather!
Teach all people. Submerge them in the atmosphere of
God, in the life of God the Father, the Son, and the Holy
Spirit" (Mt. 28:18–20). But man's task, like woman's, is
always bound together with the task of the church.

Both Paul and Peter point out that man is the head
of woman, not in himself but in Christ (1 Cor. 11:3).
This does not mean that the man is "higher"; the fact that
woman is taken from man and man is born of woman
shows that they are dependent on each other in every
respect (1 Cor. 11:11–12). Again, the gifts and responsibilities of one are worth no more than those of the other;
they are simply different. In the true order of marriage,
both husband and wife will find their rightful place, but

neither will rule the other. Love and humility will rule.

It belongs to the evil of our day that both men and women avoid the responsibilities given them by God. Women rebel against the inconvenience of pregnancy and the pain of birth, and men rebel against the burden of commitment to the children they father and to the woman who bears them. Such rebellion is a curse on our time. It will lead future generations astray. Woman was designed by God to have children, and a true man will respect and love his wife all the more because of this. Peter admonishes us:

> You husbands must conduct your married life with understanding: pay honor to the woman's body, not only because it is weaker, but also because you share together in the grace of God which gives you life. Then your prayers will not be hindered (1 Pet. 3:7).

It is clear that the difference between man and woman is not absolute. In a true woman there is courageous manliness, and in a true man there is the submission and humility of Mary. Yet because the man is the head, in a true marriage he will give the lead, even if he is a very weak person. This must not be taken as if man were an overlord and woman his servant. If a man does not lead in love and humility – if he does not lead in the spirit of Jesus – his headship will become tyranny. The head has its place in the body, but it does not dominate.

At weddings in our Bruderhof communities the bridegroom is always asked if he is willing to lead his wife "in everything that is good," which simply means to lead her more deeply to Jesus. In the same way, the bride is asked if she is willing to follow her husband. It is simply a matter of both of them following Jesus together.

TRUE LEADERSHIP MEANS LOVING SERVICE

In his letter to the Ephesians, Paul points to the self-sacrificing love that lies in true leadership: "Husbands, love your wives, just as Christ loved the church and gave himself up for her" (Eph. 5:25). This task, the task of loving, is actually the task of every man and woman, whether married or not.

When we take Paul's words to heart, we will experience the true inner unity of a relationship ruled by love – an inner speaking of the heart to God from both partners together. Only then will God's blessing rest on our marriages. We will constantly seek our beloved one anew and continually look for ways to serve each other in love. Most wonderful of all, we will find everlasting joy. As the church father Tertullian writes:

> Who can describe the happiness of a marriage contracted in the presence of the church and sealed with its blessing? What a sweet yoke it is which here joins two believing people in one hope, one way of life, one vow of loyalty, and one service to God! They are brother and sister, both busy in the same service, with no separation of soul and body,

but as two in one flesh. And where there is one
flesh, there is one spirit also. Together they pray,
together they kneel down: the one teaches the
other, and bears with the other. They are joined
together in the church of God, joined at the Lord's
table, joined in anxiety, persecution, and recovery.
They vie with each other in the service of their
Lord. Christ sees and hears, and joyfully does he
send them his peace, for where two are gathered
together in his name, there is he in the midst of
them.[15]

CHAPTER 10

THE SACREDNESS
OF SEX

Marriage should be honored by all, and the marriage bed
kept pure, for God will judge the adulterer and all the sexually
immoral (Heb. 13:4).

There are two great dangers in sex: on the one
hand, fear of the self-surrender or closeness that
a physical relationship requires, and fear that sex
is dirty and shameful; on the other, unbridled lust and
sin. Clearly, the sexual sphere is not incorruptible. Even
in marriage its potential blessings become dangers if it is
entered in isolation from God, who created it. Instead
of passion there is naked lust, instead of tenderness there
is aggression and even brutality, and instead of mutual
self-giving there is uncontrollable desire.

The church should never be silent about this (1 Cor.
5:1–5). The spirit of impurity is always waiting to tempt
us, and it will slip into the sanctuary of marriage whenever we open the door to it. Once impurity has entered
a marriage, it becomes more and more difficult to keep

focused on God's love, and easier and easier to bypass one another and succumb to evil temptations.

We must never underestimate the power of the impure spirits that drive people to do evil, even within marriage. Once under their control, sex quickly loses its nobler qualities and deteriorates into something cheap. What was created as a wonderful gift from God becomes a sinister, life-destroying experience. Only repentance can bring about healing and restoration.

THROUGH THE MARRIAGE ACT, AN UNPARALLELED UNITING CAN TAKE PLACE

We can recognize the true nature of the sexual sphere most clearly when we can see its sacredness as the fulfillment of wedded love sanctioned by God. It is the same with the act of sexual intercourse itself, the moment in which marital love comes to its fullest physical expression. Because intercourse is such a powerfully dramatic experience, it is vital that it be anchored in God. If sex is not recognized as a gift from God and subordinated to him, it can become an idol. Entered with reverence, however, it "awakens that which is most intimate, most sacred, most vulnerable in the human heart."[16]

In a true marriage, sex is guided by more than the desires of each partner: it is guided by the love that binds both partners together. When each partner gives himself in complete surrender to the other, a uniting of unparalleled depth takes place. It will not be just "physical love"; it will be the expression and fulfillment of total love, an act of unconditional giving and deep fulfillment.

It is a remarkable and wonderful experience to give oneself physically to another person. Orgasm, the climax or peak of physical uniting, is a powerful and shaking experience and has a forceful effect on the spirit. Here, the experience of the body is so forceful that it is difficult to distinguish it from the experience of the spirit. In rhythmic harmony of heart and body, two human beings reach the highest peak of the joy of love. In total union, both are lifted out of their own personalities and joined in the closest community possible. At the moment of climax a person is, so to speak, swept away – swallowed up so completely that the sense of being an independent person is momentarily submerged.

PHYSICAL UNION SHOULD ALWAYS EXPRESS UNITY OF HEART AND SOUL

We can never have too much reverence for the marriage act. Even if we reject prudishness, a feeling of reticence will make us wary of speaking about it to others. Of course, a man and woman united in marriage must be able to talk openly with each other, even about the most intimate things. But they will never do this without the reverence that springs from their love for each other.

It is of prime importance that a couple does not go to bed at night without having turned first to Jesus. It is not necessary to use many words; Jesus always knows what we mean and what we need. We must not only thank him but also seek his guidance – if we do not knock at his door, he cannot guide us. The same, of course, is true at the start of the day.

If our marriage is grounded in Jesus and his love and purity, we will find the right relationship to each other on every level. Here we must heed Paul's warning, "If you are angry, do not let your anger lead you into sin; do not let the sun go down on your anger, and do not give a foothold to the devil" (Eph. 4:26–27). Prayer is crucial in reconciling the differences that arise in the marriage relationship. To unite physically when there is no unity of spirit is hypocrisy. It is a desecration of the bond of love.

Physical uniting should always express the full uniting of spirit and soul; it should never be a means of bodily satisfaction alone. In Jesus, every physical act of love is a mutual giving of self, a sign of resolve to live for one another. It has nothing to do with power or the idea of sex as conquest.

Anyone who uses his partner merely to satisfy himself insults his own dignity and the dignity of his partner. He is using sex for a selfish purpose. This is why the Bible regards it as sin when a man withdraws from his wife before climax and allows his semen to "fall on the earth" (Gen. 38:9–10). Of course, if this happens against his will, prematurely, or in a dream, then it is not a sin. For the same reason, oral and anal intercourse are also sinful. Because they are driven only by the selfish desire for sexual excitement, these forms of sex are in reality forms of mutual masturbation.

TRUE SEXUAL FULFILLMENT IS FOUND
IN MUTUAL SUBMISSION

Sexual desire may be relatively dormant in a newly married couple, especially when neither partner has engaged in premarital sex or been addicted to masturbation. In fact, a husband may even need to awaken the urge for intercourse in his bride. Because this may take time, he should be very patient and initiate sexual union only when his wife is ready. For a virgin, the first intercourse can be painful and may cause minor bleeding. This is no cause for alarm, yet a husband should be aware of his wife's discomfort.

A true husband will have enough love for his wife to consider her state of readiness and not hurry intercourse because of his own impatience. Because he is concerned not merely with his own satisfaction, he will be sensitive to the fact that often more time is needed for a woman to reach climax than for a man, and after intercourse, he will not go happily to sleep while his wife lies awake with feelings of deep disappointment or frustration.

The sexual happiness of a woman is often more dependent than a man's on the accompanying circumstances of their union; on the unity she feels between herself and her husband, and in little acts of kindness or affectionate words. It does not consist only in the climax. Simply being together with her beloved may give her the deepest sense of fulfillment.

A couple should not be afraid to prepare one another for physical union. Loving stimulation is a strong affirma-

tion of mutual unity, and in addition to increasing readiness, it nurtures confidence and envelops a couple with
a feeling of security. Both husband and wife must learn
what pleases and stimulates their partner. Writing about
women, for instance, von Gagern says, "There are areas
of the body that are especially responsive to fondling –
the mouth, the breasts, under the arms, the spine – but
a couple's own unique love for each other will continually guide them anew."[17]

AS SELF-DISCIPLINE, ABSTINENCE CAN
DEEPEN A COUPLE'S LOVE

Physically, intercourse is always possible, but a husband
should be ready to abstain for the sake of his wife's
health, especially before and after she gives birth. In our
Bruderhof communities we recommend abstinence during
menstruation and for at least six weeks before the birth of
a child. After a birth, couples should abstain as long as
they are able, so that the mother can recover both physically and emotionally. Because every couple is different,
it is hard to suggest a time frame; the important thing is
consideration. If a husband is truly considerate of his
wife, he will be willing to discipline himself by abstaining
as long as possible (1 Thess. 4:3–5). In such times of
abstinence, out of love for her husband, the woman must
be careful not to arouse him sexually.

Naturally, the love between man and wife – between
two who live together, sleep together, and belong together – will make it much harder for them to abstain

than for a single person. All the more, they must be on guard against coming close to one another in a sexual way and then avoiding intercourse.

As a woman approaches middle-age, it is not unusual for her joy or interest in sexual intercourse to diminish. This can be hard for the man, yet he must see that his love for his wife does not decrease. Wives, for their part, should give themselves in love to their husbands as they are able, even if their joy in doing so is not the same as it was in earlier years (1 Cor. 7:3–4). Otherwise a husband may be tempted to seek other outlets for his sexual impulses. The main thing is that there is always unity of spirit and soul before physical uniting and that, when abstinence is necessary, it does not become an occasion for love to grow cold. Paul writes:

> Do not deprive each other except by mutual consent and for a time, so that you may devote yourselves to prayer. Then come together again so that Satan will not tempt you because of your lack of self-control (1 Cor. 7:5).

Abstinence, then, should always be approached with fasting and prayer – as a self-discipline. When willingly accepted in this way, it can unite a couple more deeply than ever.

In the end, everything in a marriage depends on the commitment of both partners to Jesus and on their willingness to follow his leading. Couples should remember that it was God who joined them together, and only he can keep them together, especially in difficult times. Jesus says, "Whoever loses his life will gain it" (Lk. 9:24). The same is true in Christian marriage: insofar as both partners are willing to surrender themselves again and again to each other and to Christ, they will find the true fulfillment of unity and freedom.

CHAPTER 11

PARENTHOOD AND THE GIFT OF CHILDREN

Children, obey your parents in the Lord, for this is right. "Honor your father and mother so that it may go well with you and so that you may enjoy long life on the earth." Fathers, do not exasperate your children; instead, bring them up in the training and instruction of the Lord (Eph. 6:1–4).

We live in a world where the structure of family life is undergoing profound changes, in rich and poor countries alike. The concept of family as a stable, cohesive unit is fast becoming outdated. We are even afraid to define what a family is because we do not want to offend anyone.

For years, psychologists have warned of the effects of broken marriages, of teen pregnancies, of violent homes, and other social ills, but their warnings have been given in vain. Now we are reaping a bitter harvest. All this makes it more urgent than ever for us to rediscover God's original intent in creating man and woman, and in blessing them with children.

HAVING CHILDREN TODAY REQUIRES COURAGE

Modern society despises the family. It is difficult for a
family with several children to find a house, and in many
places it is impossible to rent an apartment, even if there
is only one child. Children are simply not wanted. Many
people think it regrettable to leave jobs or other pursuits
to have children, and they often look down on women
who choose to stay at home to raise children instead of
pursuing a more "acceptable" career.

Having children in these times certainly takes great
courage, but that is what faith means: not knowing what
lies ahead, and yet still trusting that God has his hand
over all things and will have the final say. More than ever,
parents need to trust God. The health of a society (and
the health of any church or movement within society)
depends on the strength of its marriages. Where there is
reverence for God, there are strong and stable families,
but as soon as this is lost, there is rapid disintegration and
decline.

Those who know what it means to see a child smile
for the first time, to love him or her, and to feel love in
return know something of the greatness of God and the
nearness of eternity in each child. They know that their
child is like no other, and that no child could replace
this one in their hearts. They will also realize what an
awe-inspiring responsibility it is to bring a child into the
world – a responsibility that only grows with the child –

and will sense that they are too weak and sinful to bring up even one child in their own strength.

But our recognition of inadequacy should not lead us to despair. It should make us realize how dependent we are on grace. Only the adult who stands like a child before the grace of God is fit to raise a child.

ON WHAT BASIS SHOULD A FAMILY BE BUILT?

If we think of starting a family, our first question should be: on what foundation? Complete dedication to Christ and his church is the only dependable foundation. On him alone can we build a rich and fulfilled family life that will withstand the forces that attack it from outside.

It is the task of every couple to bring up their children on God's behalf, to represent the creator. For the small child especially, father and mother stand for God. That is why the commandment to honor father and mother is so vital to the upbringing of every child from the start. Without it, the commandment to honor God has no real meaning. Actually, every child has an instinctive longing for the security of father, mother, and God. It is terrible, then, when parents do not fulfill this longing, when they see parenting merely as a role and are not truly fathers or mothers. Children will sense such hypocrisy wherever it occurs, and they will become resentful, bitter, and rebellious as they grow older.

The same is true if a couple lives in dissension – if a woman does not support her husband's task as head of the family, for example, or if a man does not love and honor his wife. When children cannot find a picture of God in their parents, they have trouble finding a secure and healthy foundation for their later lives. They may even experience emotional difficulties.

It is of greatest importance that from the first day of a child's life he or she is surrounded by love and by reverence for God. To the same degree that children experience the love their parents have for each other, they will find the inner security they need in order to develop and grow.

In questions of discipline, it is best if a husband and wife are fully agreed as to what they expect in terms of behavior. Children should not have to decide which parent is right. Their position should be one of trust, not judgment. They look for consistent boundaries and for the security that comes from unity, love, and mutual respect. These things are the basis of true love for children.

CHILDREN NEED LIVING EXAMPLES, NOT RELIGIOUS WORDS

The first five years of a child's life are the most formative, and therefore the best time for parents to bring Jesus and the gospel alive to their children. This can be done quite simply: by telling them about Jesus' birth, death, and resurrection. All these things can move the hearts of children at a surprisingly young age and awaken in them a love for God and for Jesus.

We cannot bring our children to Jesus, however, if he
is only a figure in our Bibles. Children will always want
to come to Jesus, but they will instinctively rebel against
false piety. As Blumhardt once put it, "If we try to drag
children into the kingdom by means of our religiosity,
they will flee from our pious homes as fast as they are
able."[18] Therefore we should be careful not to put our
children under any religious pressure or plague them
with talk about sins they can neither understand nor com-
mit. We want them to have a childlike attitude toward
God, toward Jesus, and toward the Bible. It is of no use,
for instance, to make children learn even the shortest
passages of Scripture if God does not speak directly into
their little hearts. Rather than try to "teach" children faith,
it is much better for their parents to live their faith by
example in a spontaneous, genuine way. When our children see that we, their parents, rely on God for everything – when they see us thank him and obey his
commands – they will feel an inner urge to pray and to
follow him of their own accord.

OUR TASK IS TO GUIDE OUR CHILDREN, NOT CONTROL THEM

Raising children requires daily discipline, but we should
never forget that caring for them in God's stead means
guiding, not controlling, them. Children must be encouraged to overcome themselves and look beyond their little
worlds from a very early age, and they must learn love

and respect for others. They cannot be left to swing with every mood and follow every selfish whim without restraint. Clear directions and consistent boundaries are always necessary. In fact, discipline is the greatest love we can show them (Heb. 12:10–11). But it is never loving to coerce or crush them.

We must remember that every child is a thought of God (Psa. 139:13–17) and try to understand why it is said that "a little child will lead them" (Isa. 11:6). In guiding our children, we cannot and should not try to shape them according to our own intentions or plans. We should not force on them anything that has not been born into them, awakened from within, or given them by God. God has a specific intent for each child; he has a plan for every one, and he will hold to it. Our task is to help each child find *God's* purpose for him and fulfill it.

Carrying out this task means continually exercising self-denial in our own human efforts to lead a child. Sometimes, it may mean refraining from tearing children away from their own thoughts. Blumhardt notes how quickly we hurt our relationship with children when we interrupt their thoughts and happy disposition and attempt to influence them by our ideas or advice: "When left undisturbed, children learn obedience and respect best of all."[19]

Naturally, we must be on guard against permissiveness. Flabbiness is usually a fruit of an unhealthy emotionalism between parent and child, and it inhibits the

childlike spirit because it subjects the child to the spine-
lessness of an adult who has lost the clarity of Christ. We
must always watch that our children are free from such
false ties.

TRUE AUTHORITY STRENGTHENS
AND STIMULATES A CHILD

Children must never feel ill-used if spoken to or admon-
ished sharply. They need to learn to take themselves in
hand and face up to what has happened when they are
shown to be in the wrong. They should not give half-
answers that could mean this or that. Yet even if a certain
sharpness toward children is healthy, impatience is not,
especially when it results in corporal punishment. That,
Eberhard Arnold writes, is a "declaration of bankruptcy."

   We reject both the harshness of physical punishment
and the power of manipulation: both are forms of author-
itarianism that fail to take the child seriously as a bearer
of God's image. The one fails in mercy, and the other in
honesty. Both fail in love. True authority stimulates and
strengthens what is good in each child by leading him to
make his own decisions between right and wrong. Only
when we lead children by trusting them and loving them
will they feel the desire to struggle against the evil that
tries to work in them and us.

   Most fathers and mothers do not intentionally mislead
their children. In fact, not only their children but also
they themselves suffer when they fail to be true parents

on God's behalf. Every couple can find God's guidance and forgiveness by seeking it in prayer and by turning for help to brothers and sisters whom they trust. Entrusting the education of a child to the church in this way must never be done at the expense of the relationship between parent and child. In our Bruderhof communities, however, where we have our own teachers, we find that it often strengthens this relationship because it gives the child the security of a love that is far deeper and stronger than that of one single family. Ultimately, of course, it is not we who can raise our children, but God. My father writes in this regard:

> Christ calls us to become like children, and this means we must drop everything and become completely dependent on God and on one another. If we as parents love God with all our heart and soul, our children will have the right reverence for us, and we will also have reverence for our children and for the wonderful mystery of becoming and being a child. Reverence for the spirit that moves between parent and child is the basic element of a true family life.[20]

CHAPTER 12

THE PURITY
OF CHILDHOOD

Whoever becomes humble like this child is the greatest in the kingdom of heaven. Whoever welcomes one such child in my name welcomes me. If any of you put a stumbling block before one of these little ones who believes in me, it would be better for you if a great millstone were fastened around your neck and you were drowned in the depth of the sea (Mt. 18:4–6).

J esus' words tell us what great value the soul of a little child has in the eyes of God. Spiritually, every child is close to the throne of God, to the heart of God, and every child has a guardian angel who "always sees the face of the Father in heaven" (Mt. 18:10).

When a baby comes into the world it is as though he or she brings the pure air of heaven along. At every birth we feel that something of God is born, that something of eternity has come down to us. The innocence of a child is an enormous blessing.

THE CHILDLIKE SPIRIT MUST BE PROTECTED –
BUT ALSO NURTURED

In spite of the innocence of every child, however, there is also an inclination to sin in each one (Prov. 22:15). That is why it is such a terrible sin to lead a child astray. Children are corrupted not only by intentionally misleading them to sin, but by exposing them to anything that violates the atmosphere of innocence around them and deprives them of their childlikeness. So many of the images to which children are exposed today – at home on television, at shopping malls, and at school – are created by adults obsessed with sex, violence, power, and money. Is it any wonder that they lose their childlike spirit and childhood itself while they are still children?

The best thing we can do for our children is to see that the whole atmosphere in which they live is filled with the spirit of purity and ruled by love. The inner education of children – the task of leading them to respect and to love God, their parents, their teachers, and everyone around them – is a holy privilege. Here it is of utmost importance that we pray for God's spirit to arouse our children's wills for what is pure, genuine, and good. Guiding children to do what is good is far more important than teaching them to recite verses or to say prayers which may not come from the heart. In our communities, we generally avoid formal religious instruction as such. We feel that children

can learn to love God best through simple songs and
through stories from the Bible, and through the daily
example of adults around them who love each other.

In leading children to Jesus it is important that we
ourselves have a childlike attitude toward his commandments and sayings, toward the angel-world, and toward
the Bible as a whole. How very quickly and simply children take these things into their hearts!

We can also bring our children to God through the
world around them, by helping them to sense him in all
they see – in sun, moon, and stars; birds and animals;
trees and flowers; mountains and thunderstorms. Every
child wants to live in nature and with nature, and in
every child there is a love for the earth, a joy in the starry
sky, and a warm fondness for everything living. Most
wonderful of all, every child firmly trusts that a creator
is above and behind it all (Psa. 19:1–2). To a child, the
world of God and his angels is often much closer and
more real than we suspect.

Through creation and through the Bible, children
will encounter suffering and death at an early age. While
it is important for us to teach them to have a heart for
those who suffer, it is equally important not to burden or
frighten them. In general, too many facts about the cycle
of life – of reproduction, birth, and death – can harm a
child's inner experience of God's world. Birth and death
are mysteries that can only be understood in relationship
to God, and there is danger of irreverence in saying
too much. Concerning sex, especially, it is simply not

necessary for a child or even an adolescent to know everything. It is all too easy to destroy the sacredness and mystery of life with too much discussion.

I am not in any way suggesting that children be brought
up ignorant of the basic facts of life. I only mean that these
things should never be separated from the world of God.
The main thing is that we do not disturb the purity of
childhood – the natural relationship of every child to his
or her creator.

EDUCATION MEANS ROUSING A CHILD
TO CHOOSE RIGHT OVER WRONG

To protect the purity of children means to win them for
the good. It is wrong to suppose that a child is not
tempted to evil. As parents we must always be ready to
fight evil in our children, whether it takes the form of
lying, stealing, disrespect, or sexual impurity. But we must
do this without too many rules (Col. 2:20–22). Moralism,
which always involves suspicion and mistrust, ruins the
childlike spirit. On the one hand, children cannot be left
unprotected to fall prey to whatever evil comes their way.
On the other hand, we should not discourage them by
constantly haranguing them about their faults. True education does not mean molding or squelching a child with
constant criticism. It means rousing him or her to choose
right over wrong.

Even from a very early age, we must be careful not to
spoil our children. Spoiling leads to selfishness, lack of
self-control, and deep discontent; in other words, it leads

to sin. Parents who spoil their children often confuse love
with emotionalism. They think they will win their children by clinging to them, but in actual fact they only
hinder them from developing into healthy, independent
beings. To treat one's children as one's emotional property is to lack reverence for them as images of God in
their own right.

Among older children, disrespect toward peers, educators, and parents is not uncommon. Disrespect shows
itself in many ways. Often it takes the form of machismo
(which is mostly a cover-up for cowardice, and is only
displayed when others are present) or a lack of consideration for others, or irreverent or destructive behavior.
Singing may be despised as effeminate, signs of affection
to babies may be scoffed at, and everything religious or
moral is apt to be mocked. Because children who demonstrate such tendencies are insecure, they are suscep-
tible to peer pressure and will often turn to the support
of a clique. Parents and teachers need to be alert to this,
because the exclusive nature of even the friendliest clique
is never healthy. The best antidote to cliquishness is positive guidance, care, and genuine interest in each child.

EVERY CHILD INSTINCTIVELY LONGS
FOR A GOOD CONSCIENCE

The question of sexual impurity in children needs special
sensitivity and discernment. My father writes:

How to fight against sin in children is a very difficult question. If there are indecencies, for example, which mostly begin with children exposing themselves to each other and sometimes touching each other, the child will feel instinctively that this is not right. These indecencies almost always involve lying. We must be careful not to make too much of such things among children. It may only draw their attention to the sexual area all the more. The best thing, perhaps, is to admonish them and so close the matter, and then help them to think of other things.

We grown-ups too easily forget that many things do not mean the same to a child as they do to us, and we must never project our ideas and feelings and experiences onto a child's mind (Tit. 1:15). We must also never forget that it is in a certain way natural for children to go through periods of sexual curiosity. This cannot be mistaken for sin. But we should lead our children in such a way that their souls remain pure and innocent. Too much questioning can harm a child, because through fear he or she may become more and more entangled in lies.

It is a great injustice to label children or adolescents, especially those who have offended in the sexual area. In our assessment of childish offenses, we should beware of coming too quickly to harsh conclusions about a child's character or future development. Rather, we should help him or her to find new interests and to make a joyful new beginning.

We know that we can find the way to the heart
of any child by appealing to the conscience. Every
child has an instinctive, heartfelt longing for a pure
conscience, and we should support this longing
so that he or she does not suffer from a burdened
conscience.

There is a certain point at which children are no
longer children in the true sense of the word. The
moment they sin consciously, they cease to be children. It is then the task of parents and teachers to
help them find repentance, the experience of Jesus
on the cross, and a conversion that leads to the
forgiveness of sins. Through the cross a lost childhood *can* be restored.[21]

PURITY, LIKE IMPURITY, IS LEARNED BY EXAMPLE

For parents, the importance of seeking a relationship of
trust with their children from earliest childhood cannot be
emphasized enough. We cannot wait for problems that
may only arise around the age of five or six. If we do not
build relationships with our children while they are still
young, we may never gain the trust and respect necessary
to solve the more serious problems that will come with
adolescence.

The years between thirteen and twenty-one are especially crucial, of course, since it is during these years that
children become increasingly aware of their sexuality.
How easy it is for parents – and whole churches – to turn

a blind eye to the teenagers right in front of them and to
fail them miserably simply by ignoring them. How different our American high schools would be if parents took
time for their teenagers! Plenty of parents warn them
about alcohol, drugs, and sexual experimentation, but
how many take time on a regular basis to guide their
children's interests and encourage them to use their time
creatively, to do more than watch the latest videos or
hang out at the mall? Committed parents will remain in
close contact with their children throughout the ups and
downs of adolescence. Fathers will be not only fathers to
their children, but also comrades and friends; mothers
will be the same.

Young people always need someone to confide in.
Whether it is a parent, pastor, counselor, or friend, there
must be someone they trust with whom they can freely
share their joys or struggles, and with whom they can talk
openly about sex without shame or embarrassment.

Purity, like impurity, is learned first and foremost by
example (Tit. 2:6–8). Children need to see that the love
between their parents is indissoluble, and to know that
certain looks, touches, and words of affection are appro-
priate only between a married man and woman. They
need to see that physical intimacy belongs to marriage
alone and that experimentation of any sort beforehand
will only stain a later marriage. They certainly need to be
spared the confusion and pain of broken relationships
and sexual sin in or among adults around them.

That is why it is so important that the church has a
central place in family life. Children must be able to see
living examples of purity not only in their parents, but in
everyone around them, whether married or single.

THE BEST SAFEGUARD AGAINST SIN IS LOVE

Purity can never be fostered in a vacuum. Our children
and youth need to gain a heart for Jesus and his cause of
peace and social justice. When their hearts are filled with
God and inspired for his cause, they will instinctively
react against evil. When we lead them to recognize the
needs of others, they will long to reach out in love. The
idea that children have no social conscience, no feeling
for the suffering, injustice, and guilt of our world is simply not true – this can only happen if they are brought up
in an artificial environment that revolves around their
own comfort and pleasure. When genuine children come
face to face with the need of others, or when they see
others reaching out to the needy, they will have an inner
urge to extend their own love in practical ways.

The best safeguard against sin is always love. Love
binds together all the virtues in perfect unity (Col. 3:14).
Love is the message we need to bring to our children and
youth, most importantly by demonstrating love in everything we ourselves say and do. So many young people
today live for themselves and for their own interests.
They work hard to get good grades, to excel in sports, to
win the recognition earned by a scholarship – all of which

is commendable. But how many of them care about their neighbors or the need of the world around them? We need to challenge and stretch our youth to interact with others, especially with others of different faiths and backgrounds.

Often parents try to protect their teenagers by anxiously shielding them from situations of impurity or violence, especially at high school or in college. Yet perhaps what they really need is the opposite: the opportunity to stand on their own feet and witness to what they themselves – not just their parents – believe.

Our children need to reach out and learn what others of their time are thinking and feeling. They need to relate to their peers and to the burning social, political, and economic issues of their day. They need to have a heart for the despair of those who have turned to drugs and alcohol, and for those who suffer from abusive relationships in the home. Without the ability to understand and relate to others outside their sphere, they will have no real connection to the world around them and will never be given the opportunity to test their own convictions.

We will never raise perfect children, but we firmly believe that it is possible to raise children who will respond to our guidance and discipline, in spite of the terrible corruption and darkness of our age (Prov. 22:6). As long as we are able to maintain a relationship of mutual respect and reverence, we will find the way forward with our children. It will cost a fight, sometimes a serious one, yet for the sake of a child's soul, a battle is always worthwhile. Naturally, our children may grow up to choose a path of life different from that which we would have chosen for them. But if we pray to Jesus for his guidance every day, we can be confident that he will lead us and them.

CHAPTER 13

FOR THOSE CONSIDERING MARRIAGE

Train yourself to be godly. For physical training is of some value, but godliness has value for all things, holding promise for both the present life and the life to come...Don't let anyone look down on you because you are young, but set an example in speech, in life, in love, in faith, and in purity (1 Tim. 4:8,12).

I t is shocking how casually, and with what selfishness and naiveté, young men and women today plunge into relationships and even into marriage. Yet how should young people handle the natural attractions and friendships that develop between them? What is the godly approach? How can young men and women stay clear of the superficial eroticism of our time and find truly free and natural relationships? And how can they best prepare themselves for the responsibilities and demands of marriage?

CONVENTIONAL DATING CHEAPENS
THE MEANING OF COMMITMENT

We should rejoice when there are friendships between young men and women, and when there are opportunities for positive mutual exchanges in their daily lives. To have fear of what might go wrong among them is wholly unnatural and a sign of mistrust. Young people need opportunities to relate to each other in group settings where they can work, share, sing, or relax together. To pair off or form exclusive relationships is unhealthy and out of place: in the church, young men and women should get to know each other first as brothers and sisters. They must have the freedom to be seen together without being subjected to all sorts of gossip or speculation about their friendship. The pressure caused by such talk inhibits freedom. It skews and undermines everything that is good in a relationship.

It is typical of the immaturity of a young person to "fall in love" first with one and then with another, like a bee going from flower to flower. It is only natural to want to search for "the right one"; but the church cannot tolerate the continual forming and then dissolving of new relationships. The casual attitude of a young man or woman who flits from one boyfriend or girlfriend to the next is never right. It dulls the conscience and cheapens the meaning of commitment. The waves of emotional attraction that accompany every friendship between a boy and a girl are perfectly normal, but if they are not placed under Christ, they can leave wounds that may last a lifetime.

Because of this, we reject conventional dating in our communities. For the most part, dating in our society has become a game – a ritual of pairing off with a boyfriend or a girlfriend on the basis of physical and emotional attraction. It is built on a false understanding of friendship and often has little to do with genuine love or faithfulness. In many instances, dating is centered on an unhealthy preoccupation with personal "image." And when it involves sex, it can leave a conscience so heavily burdened that it takes years to heal.

Vanity and superficiality go hand in hand with conventional dating. So does flirting – drawing attention to oneself so as to sexually attract another person. Flirting demonstrates inner insecurity and unhappiness, and it is an insult to God.

MUTUAL FEELINGS ARE NOT SUFFICIENT FOR BUILDING A LASTING RELATIONSHIP

How should a young man or woman find the right partner? For a Christian the decisive factor should always be unity of heart and soul in the Spirit. Both partners must feel that their relationship leads them closer to Jesus, for his will alone can bring together two people who are meant for each other. Without Jesus and the special unity he gives between two people, a couple will very likely not survive the storms and struggles that are a part of every marriage, especially once they have children.

Even when a young couple is sure that they want to enter a more committed relationship, through engagement, for instance, they should test their love for a time to see whether it is merely the straw fire of romantic attraction, or whether there is something deeper. Obviously, they will feel emotional desire, but that can never be the deciding factor in making a commitment. The real question to each partner should always be, "What is God's will for my life and future?" Again, physical and emotional attractions are natural, but they do not provide sufficient ground on which to marry or found a family. A relationship based only on these is a shallow one, and eventually it will go to pieces. Faith in Jesus is the surest basis.

If faith is the only firm foundation for Christian marriage, it follows that each partner must make a commitment to Christ and the church before making a commitment to each other. Here the importance of baptism cannot be emphasized enough. As a confession of repentance for sin and as the covenant of a clear conscience with God, baptism is one of the greatest gifts a person can experience. I would even say that without it, there is no secure foundation for a Christian marriage.

Of course, no one should be baptized for the sake of husband, wife, or children (Lk. 14:26). Nor should the desire for baptism be mixed with feelings of desire for a potential marriage partner. If baptism is to have real meaning, it must be the seal of deep repentance, conversion, and faith.

A HEALTHY RELATIONSHIP
NEEDS TIME AND CARE

Jesus says that we cannot serve two masters (Mt. 6:24).
He teaches us that when we trust God alone, and trust
him completely, he will provide for all our needs, including the need for a partner. "Seek first the kingdom of God
and his righteousness, and all these things will be given
to you as well" (Mt. 6:33). This advice is important not
only for those who might be preoccupied with the question of marriage in an unhealthy way, but for all of us.

I would never expect a young person to give up marriage like the Apostle Paul did; the call to celibacy must be
felt from within. But unless marriage is God's will (and this
is often difficult to discern) every one of us should be willing to give it up (Phil. 3:8). When the light of Jesus breaks
into our life, we will find strength to surrender to him so
radically that everything will find its true proportion.

Contrary to the widely accepted belief that the healthiest
relationship is the most private one, we feel that engagement and marriage are concerns of the whole church, not
just of the individuals involved. Therefore, when young
men and women in our communities feel drawn to one
another, they turn first to their parents and ministers. From
this moment on their relationship is placed under the care
of the church. Our young people do not regard this step
as an imposition, nor do they feel they are being chaper-
oned. On the contrary, they are grateful for the possibility
of guidance in an area where immaturity and impurity
bring misery to so many.

It is vital that a couple wishing to marry in the fear
of God takes time to get to know each other inwardly,
and to discover all there is of God in each other. There
are plenty of wholesome activities a couple can find for
this purpose: reading, hiking, visiting each other's families, or participating in a community service project
together. Writing to each other is also a good way to become acquainted on a deeper level. At first, correspon-
dence should be non-binding – as from brother to sister
and vice versa. Emotional appeals about romantic love
and belonging together have no place at this stage. They
would only obscure the discernment necessary to decide
whether or not a future commitment is really God's will.

In our communities we encourage our young couples
to share their letters with their parents or minister and
ask them for guidance. Naturally, this does not mean that
our ministers control the relationship or its outcome –
but they do provide input, support, and spiritual guidance. One can only wonder how many marriages might
be saved if young couples everywhere had the humility
to turn to their parents (or another older couple they
trust) for advice, even if not in this specific way.

Again, a healthy relationship cannot be rushed. Like
a flower, it must be allowed to open in God's time, not
forced in hopes of an early bloom. If a marriage is to
last, it must be built on a carefully laid foundation.

WHAT MATTERS MOST, IN THE DECISION
TO MARRY, IS GOD'S WILL

Honesty is fundamental to every true relationship. If a couple does not feel that they are growing closer to each other and to God, they must be open about it. Here the church, too, must care enough about its members to be honest with them – to help a couple discern if they are really meant for one another, and to consider whether their friendship is bearing good fruit. Even if no promise has been made, ending a relationship is painful. But better a painful end than the endless pain of a relationship that leads nowhere.

Only when two young people, independently of each other but with the input of their parents and minister, feel assured over a period of time that they really belong together for life are they ready to become engaged. Only when they feel in the depth of their hearts that their partner is *the* person meant for them, and that it is God alone who has led them together, are they truly ready to make a bond for life.

Once engaged, most couples want to participate fully in their love and express it actively in giving and receiving. Their hearts are set on making each other as happy and fulfilled as possible, and they feel ready to do anything to bring this about. All the more, such couples must realize that the powers of love are much greater than they themselves, and they must ask God daily for the strength to discipline themselves.

Long embraces, caressing, mouth-to-mouth kissing, and anything else that might lead to sexual arousal should be avoided. The desire for physical closeness between two is natural, but instead of revolving around this desire, an engaged couple should focus on getting to know each other more intimately on an inner level and nurturing each other's love to Jesus and the church.

A marriage that starts with a conscience burdened by unconfessed sin is a marriage without a stable foundation, and it can be set right only through confession and repentance. The health of a marriage depends on the ground in which it grows. If it is sown in the soil of purity and faith, it will bear good fruit and have God's blessing.

Try to grasp the spirit, not the letter, of what I have written. Seek one another's innermost heart, and turn to Christ in absolute trust to seek his answer to every question. He will never fail to lead you clearly.

CHAPTER 14

THE SERVICE
OF SINGLENESS

The disciples said to him, "If that is the situation between a husband and wife, it is better not to marry." To this Jesus replied,
"That is something which not everyone can accept, but only
those for whom God has appointed it. For while some are inca-
pable of marriage because they were born so, or were made so
by men, there are others who have themselves renounced marriage for the sake of the kingdom of heaven. Let those accept it
who can" (Mt. 19:10–12).

The gift of unity, whether with other people or
with God, does not depend in any way on marriage. In fact, the New Testament teaches that a
deeper dedication to Christ may be found by giving up
marriage for the sake of the kingdom of God. Those who
renounce everything for Jesus, including the gift of marriage, are given a great promise by him: he will be especially near to them at his return (Rev. 14:1–5). Whether
such people find themselves without a life partner because of abandonment, death, or lack of opportunity,
they can find a much greater calling than marriage if they

are able to accept their singleness in the depth of their
hearts. They can dedicate their lives in a special way to
undivided service for God's kingdom.

TO LIVE FULLY IS TO LIVE FOR CHRIST

Every man and every woman on earth who desires to
follow Christ must be completely transformed by him.
This challenge takes on a deeper meaning for those
who are single (for whatever reason) and who carry their
singleness for Christ's sake. Such a person will find a
special relationship to him.

A life lived for Christ is life in its fullest sense
(Jn.10:10). We must never forget this; it is our deepest
calling. If we truly love Christ the Bridegroom with undivided hearts, we will be immersed in him just as we are
immersed in water at baptism. If we live in Christ, our
love for him will guide our love to our brothers and sisters and to all those around us.

The story of Francis of Assisi and his friendship with
Clare shows in a wonderful way the significance of brotherly and sisterly love – even when it does not lead to
marriage. When all of Francis's brothers and friends de-
serted him, he went to Clare. In her he had a friend he
could rely on. Even after his death she remained loyal to
him and continued to carry out his mission, despite opposition. Here was a relationship that had nothing to do
with marriage but was still genuinely intimate – a friendship of true purity and unity in God.

There will always be women and men like Clare and Francis who remain unmarried for the sake of Christ. Yet we must recognize that the gift of a relationship such as theirs is not given to everyone. In struggling for purity, most single people are no different from married people. Singleness is no safeguard against impurity – in every heart, purity requires constant watchfulness, a daily fight against the flesh, and a firm attitude against sin.

IF WE ALLOW HIM, JESUS CAN FILL EVERY VOID

The Scriptures never promise us the removal of temptation. But we do have the assurance that it need not overcome us (1 Cor.10:13). If we prove ourselves in patience and faithfulness, God will help us. This is not to say that it is possible to keep pure by the strength of our own will. Yet by the power of the Holy Spirit, and through the help of caring brothers and sisters, it is possible to find freedom and victory (Gal. 6:1–2).

For those who do not find a partner in marriage but feel no special calling to remain single for the sake of Jesus, there is a danger of bitterness. If a deep yearning for marriage remains unfulfilled, especially over a long period of time, it can harden the heart. Then only God's grace can protect the soul and enable it to let go – to give up marriage and still find peace.

When single people give up marriage unreservedly, with their whole will, Jesus will fill the void that might otherwise burden them. They will remember how he

ended his life on the cross, and they will find joy in bearing singleness as their sacrifice for him. Those who continually long for marriage, despite the fact that God has
not given it to them, can never attain this joy. Marriage *is*
a great gift, but to belong completely and undividedly to
Christ is a greater gift.

Ultimately, we have to be willing to be used by God as
he wills and find contentment in whatever circumstances
we find ourselves (Phil. 4:11–13). We should never think
that God does not love us. Such a thought is of the devil.

Naturally, no matter how dedicated a single person
is, he or she will still experience moments, days, even
weeks, of sadness and struggle. The knowledge that marriage and children are beyond reach will always bring
pangs of longing and a sense of loss. But rather than
dwell on these things, it is better (even if harder) to look
to God and to turn to one's brothers and sisters in the
church. Bonhoeffer writes:

> Pain is a holy angel who shows us treasures that
> would otherwise remain forever hidden; through
> him men and women have become greater than
> through all the joys of the world. It must be so and
> I tell myself this in my present situation over and
> over again. The pain of suffering and of longing,
> which can often be felt even physically, must be
> there, and we cannot and need not talk it away.
> But it needs to be overcome every time, and thus
> there is an even holier angel than the one of pain;
> that is, the one of joy in God.[22]

SINGLENESS CAN BE ACCEPTED AS A BURDEN –
OR AS A HIGHER CALLING

Single men and women must never fall into the trap
of estranging themselves from life and love in bitterness.
They must not stifle what is best in themselves or give
themselves over to dreams or to desires that cannot be
satisfied. They must not let self-circling fantasies block
the unfolding of all that God has given them. If they are
able to accept their singleness as a gift or a special calling, they will let none of their energy or love go unused.
Their longings will be fulfilled in giving: in a stream of
love that moves away from themselves, and toward Christ
and the church. As Paul says:

> An unmarried man is concerned about the Lord's
> affairs – how he can please the Lord. But a married
> man is concerned about the affairs of this world –
> how he can please his wife – and his interests are
> divided. An unmarried woman or virgin is con-
> cerned about the Lord's affairs: her aim is to be
> devoted to the Lord in both body and spirit. But a
> married woman is concerned about the affairs of
> this world – how she can please her husband. I am
> saying this for your own good, not to restrict you,
> but that you may live in a right way in undivided
> devotion to the Lord (1 Cor. 7:32–35).

Earlier in the same letter, Paul refers to another blessing
of singleness: the lack of care and worry over spouse and
children, especially in times of hardship. "Those who

marry will have pain and grief in this bodily life, and my
aim is to spare you" (1 Cor. 7:28).

Widows, like the unmarried, are also able to serve the
church and the needy at times when a married person
could not. Paul says, "A woman who is really widowed
and left without anybody can give herself up to God
in hope and consecrate all her days and nights to peti-
tions and meetings for prayer" (1 Tim. 5:5). In the early
church in Jerusalem, widows were appointed to serve
the poor or entrusted with other responsibilities. "In even
the smallest church community the overseer had to be
a friend to the poor, and there had to be at least one
widow responsible to see to it, day and night, that no
sick or needy person was neglected."[23]

How sad it is that today it is very often the widows –
and other single women and men – who are themselves
neglected and lonely! May the church always be ready to
meet the needs of such sisters and brothers (1 Cor. 12:26).
Especially with the collapse of the family, we must find
new ways to show single members extra love and care
and to involve them in the lives of their families or
fellowships. This does not mean pressing them to find
a spouse and then pitying them if they don't – that will
only add to their pain. It means welcoming their gifts
and services in the church, providing them with meaningful tasks, and drawing them into the inner life of the
church so that they may find fulfillment.

NO MATTER OUR STATE,
ALL OF US ARE CALLED TO LOVE

Those of us who are married should recognize that
our happiness is a gift – something to be shared and
passed on. We should want to reach out to those who
struggle with feelings of loneliness. Most important, all
of us, whether married or single, should remember that
true fulfillment and joy is found in serving one another
in the spirit of community. We are called to a love that
gives unconditionally – not to the grasping love of a cozy
marriage nor to the indulging love of isolated self-pity.

As Christians, we know that true love is found in its
most perfect form in Jesus. Many of us have been touched
by Jesus, or been called and used by him. But that is not
enough. Each of us must ask God to let us experience
him personally – in the very depths of our hearts. Our
eyes must be fixed on him and him alone so that we
can see him as he really is, and not grow weary and
lose heart (Heb. 12:2–3).

The span of life is short, and as Paul warns us, the
world in its present form is passing away (1 Cor. 7:29–31).
What we need most in our time is Christ, but not only
as a guide or an image before our eyes. He must become
a living force in our daily lives. He said, "I came on earth
to kindle a fire. How I wish it were already burning!"
(Lk. 12:49)

Where is Christ most clearly revealed as he was and
still is? We must seek for him with our brothers and sis-

ters. We must ask that he is revealed today and every day among us. More than that, we must ask for the courage to witness to him before others just as he is, with tenderness, meekness, and humility, but also in truth, clarity, and sharpness. We must not add or take away anything. That is the essence of single-heartedness, and the service of singleness.

THE SPIRIT OF OUR AGE

CHAPTER 15

WITH OR WITHOUT GOD

Be imitators of God, therefore, and live a life of love, just as Christ loved us and gave himself up for us...Among you there must not be even a hint of sexual immorality, or of any kind of impurity, or of greed, because these are improper for God's holy people. Nor should there be obscenity, foolish talk, or coarse joking...Let no one deceive you with empty words, for because of such things God's wrath comes on those who are disobedient (Eph. 5:1–6).

Throughout Scripture the covenant of God with his people and the unity of Christ with his church is compared to the union of marriage. In our culture, however, marriage – the very thing we should honor and celebrate most as love – has been attacked, dragged into the dirt, and destroyed by the spirits of impurity and irreverence.

FOR MANY PEOPLE TODAY, LOVE IS A DELUSION

The desecration of love is one of the greatest tragedies of our time. Increasingly, love is understood as nothing more than selfish desire, and the satisfaction of this desire is seen as fulfillment. People talk about sexual liberation but remain trapped in bondage to their sexual desires; they talk about true love but live in self-absorbed estrangement. Our age is a loveless age: relationships and hearts are broken everywhere, millions of human lives are discarded almost before they have begun, thousands of children are abused or abandoned, and fear and mistrust abound even in supposedly healthy marriages. Love has been reduced to mean sex. Because of this, it is nothing more than a delusion for many – short-lived intimacy followed by gnawing emptiness and anguish.

How can we rediscover the real meaning of love? So many things in the world today take away our belief in lasting and unconditional love. So much of what has to do with "love" these days really has to do with the excitement and passion of lust. We live in a sex-obsessed, sex-crazed society, and everything reeks of it – advertising, literature, fashion, and entertainment. Marriage has been the first casualty: its significance has become so distorted that its true meaning has been lost.

Of course, no honest person can lay the blame for all of this at the door of the media or of some vague force in society. Certainly, the media has confused thousands of people and left them hardened. But it is we – each

one of us – whose souls are burdened by the sin of our
own lust, whose marriages have fallen apart, whose
children have gone astray. We cannot ignore our own
misdeeds; we must take responsibility for our own
actions, for every instance where we have accepted the
spirit of impurity and let evil into our own hearts. We
have mocked and twisted the image of God and separated ourselves from our creator. We must learn to listen
again to the deepest cries of our hearts, and repent and
turn back to God.

Thirty years have passed since the beginning of the sexual
revolution, and its devastating aftermath should be obvious to anyone: widespread promiscuity; rising rates of
teen pregnancy and suicide; tens of millions of abortions;
the spread of sexually transmitted diseases; the erosion
of the family and home life; and the rise of a violent
new generation. "We have sown the wind, and reap the
whirlwind" (Hos. 8:7).

Our time grossly overestimates the importance of sex.
Whether on bookstands, in convenience stores, or at
supermarket counters, its significance is exaggerated in
a thoroughly unhealthy way. Love between man and
woman is no longer regarded as sacred or noble; it has
become a commodity seen only in an animal sense,
as an uncontrollable impulse that must be satisfied.

As a tool of the sexual revolution, modern sex education more than anything else is responsible for all this.
Sex education was supposed to bring us freedom,

enlightened attitudes, responsibility, and safety. Isn't it obvious by now that it has been a failure? Haven't we seen by now that knowledge is no safeguard, and that sex education as taught in most schools has only increased sexual activity?

TRUE EDUCATION FOR THE SEXUAL LIFE INSTILLS REVERENCE

Most parents have very little, if any, idea of what their children are taught in sex education classes. Sex education has never been a simple presentation of biological facts. In many curricula students are graphically taught (sometimes by way of films) about various sexual practices, including masturbation, and about "safe" sex. In others, sexual perversions are openly and explicitly discussed and presented as normal ways of finding sexual "fulfillment." In some school districts an appreciation and understanding for the homosexual lifestyle is encouraged: it is, our children are told, a perfectly acceptable alternative to heterosexual marriage. Some schools even have students pair off to discuss topics such as foreplay and orgasm. Antibiotics and abortion are presented as positive safety nets in case contraception and safe sex practices fail. Abstinence, if not entirely ignored, is mentioned only in passing. As William Bennett, former Secretary of Education, writes:

> There is a coarseness, a callousness, a cynicism, a banality, and a vulgarity to our time. There are too

many signs of a civilization gone rotten. And the
worst of it has to do with our children: we live in a
culture that at times seems almost dedicated to the
corruption of the young, to ensuring the loss of their
innocence before their time.[24]

In general, much of what is taught today in the name of
sex education is a horror, and as Christians we must protest against it. It is often little more than the formalized
training of irreverence, impurity, and rebellion against the
plan of God.

True education for the sexual life takes place best
between parent and child in an environment of reverence
and trust. To educate anyone about sex through anony-
mous images and impersonal information will only
awaken the sexual impulse of a child prematurely and,
in his mind, separate sex from love and commitment.

Obviously we should not be afraid to talk freely with
our own children about sexual matters, especially as they
approach adolescence. Otherwise they will learn about
these things first from their peers, and rarely in a reverent
atmosphere. All the same, there is a danger in giving a
child too many biological facts about sex. Often, a factual
approach to sex robs it of its divine mystery.

To the Christian parent, sex education means guiding
the sexual conscience of his or her children to sense
their own dignity and the dignity of others. It means helping them to understand that selfish pleasure, whether it
"hurts" anybody else or not, is contrary to love (Gal. 5:13).

It means teaching them that, separated from God, sexual intercourse or any other sexual activity burdens the conscience and undermines honest relationships. It means opening their eyes to see the deep emptiness that leads people – and could lead them too – into sexual sin.

A child can acquire a healthy attitude to his body and to sex quite naturally, simply by being taught that his body, as the temple of the Spirit, is holy, and that any defilement of it is sin. I will never forget the deep impression it made on me as a young teen when my father took me for a walk with him and told me about the struggle for a pure life and the importance of keeping myself pure for the woman I might find and marry some day. He said to me, "If you are able to live a pure life now, it will be easier for the rest of your life. But if you give in now to personal impurity, it will become harder and harder to withstand temptation, even once you marry."

ANY MISUSE OF SEX CUTS US OFF FROM OUR TRUE SELVES AND FROM EACH OTHER

Young people underestimate the power of the demonic forces they allow into their lives when they give in to impurity. Take masturbation, for example. As children grow into young men and women, their sexual desire increases, and often their most immediate urge is to seek sexual gratification through masturbation. Increasingly, parents, educators, and ministers of our day claim that masturbation is healthy and natural and that the sexual

activity it often leads to, even among children who have
barely reached puberty, is normal.

Why are we parents and educators so afraid to speak
the truth – to warn our children not only of the dangers
of promiscuity but also of masturbation? (Prov. 5:1ff.)
Aren't both illnesses of the soul? Don't both desecrate
and betray the image of God, and undermine the
marriage bond? Masturbation can never bring true satisfaction. It is a solitary act. It is self-stimulation, self-gratification, self-abuse – it closes us within a dream world and
separates us from genuine relationships. When it becomes habitual (which it often does), it aggravates isolation and loneliness. At its worst, as a breach in the bond
of unity and love for which sex is created, it is compa-
rable to adultery. I have counseled many young people
who are enslaved by masturbation: they earnestly desire
to be freed from their habit, but they fall into it again
and again.

Often enslavement to masturbation is connected to
another form of bondage: pornography. Very few people
will admit an addiction to pornography, but the fact that
it is a steadily growing billion-dollar industry shows how
widespread it is, also among "Christians."

Many people claim that pornography should not be
criminalized because it is a "victimless crime." Yet anything that encourages impurity, even in the form of solitary sexual arousal, is a crime because it degrades the
human body, which was created in God's image as a

temple of the soul (1 Cor. 6:19). The so-called lines typi-
cally drawn between pornography, masturbation, one-
night stands, and prostitution are actually an illusion.
All of them are means used to attain sexual satisfaction
without the "burden" of commitment. All reduce the mystery of sex to a technique for satisfying lust. And all of
them are shameful – the secrecy of those who indulge
in them betrays that fact more clearly than anything else
(Rom. 13:12–13).

PRAYER AND CONFESSION CAN FREE US FROM THE BURDEN OF IMPURITY

No one can free himself from impurity or any other sin
in his own strength. Freedom comes through the attitude
of inner poverty, through continually turning to God.
The struggle against temptation is in everyone and will
always be there, but through prayer and confession, sin
can be overcome.

Whenever we let down our guard in the struggle for
purity – whenever we allow passion and lust to overcome
us – we are in danger of throwing ourselves completely
away. Then we will not be able to drive away the evil
spirits we have allowed to enter, and the intervention
of Christ himself will be needed to bring freedom.
Without this, there will be only deepening hopelessness
and despair.

In the most extreme instances the desperation brought
on by a secret life of impurity ends in suicide. Suicide is

the ultimate act of rebellion against God. But it is never an answer. If we find ourselves in the abyss of despair, the only answer is to seek God and ask for his compassion and mercy. Even when we find ourselves at the end of our rope, God wants to give us new hope and courage, no matter how deeply we feel we have betrayed him. God is always ready to forgive every sin (1 Jn. 1:9); we only need to be humble enough to ask him. When someone is tempted by thoughts of suicide, the most important thing we can do is to show him love – to remind him that each of us was created by and for God, and that each of us has a purpose to fulfill.

To turn from sin and to realize that we are created for God is always a revelation and a joy. If we faithfully face God in our lifetime here on earth, we will recognize the magnitude of our wonderful task, the task of receiving his love and sharing it with others. There is no calling more wonderful.

CHAPTER 16

SHAMEFUL EVEN TO MENTION?

Live as children of light (for the fruit of the light consists in all goodness, righteousness, and truth) and find out what pleases the Lord. Have nothing to do with the fruitless deeds of darkness, but rather expose them. For it is shameful even to mention what the disobedient do in secret (Eph. 5:8–12).

In June 1995 a panel of the Church of England recommended that the phrase "living in sin" be abandoned and that unmarried couples, heterosexual and homosexual alike, be "given encouragement and support" in their lifestyles and more readily welcomed into Anglican congregations. Suggesting that "loving homosexual relations and acts" are intrinsically no less valuable than heterosexual ones, the panel proposed that love should be allowed to be expressed "in a variety of relationships."[25] Although such a statement in itself is hardly surprising in today's world, it is shocking that it should come from within an established church.

WE MUST LOVE THE SINNER, BUT WE MUST ALSO SPEAK OUT AGAINST SIN

Recently I served on a parent-teachers' committee at a local high school and was able to observe just how powerful the movement to accept homosexuality has become – how it has crept into almost every aspect of public life. The school district's Health and Safety Advisory Committee was so afraid of alienating gays and lesbians that it was hesitant even to define "family," let alone take a position on so-called family values. Finally, it settled on defining "family" as "two people with a commitment."

Many politicians and an increasing number of clergy are afraid to say anything against such a definition for fear of losing voter support or their jobs. Very few dare to stand in opposition and say, "enough!" But by refusing to define marriage as a covenant between one man and one woman, they not only call into question the entire institution of the family but flatly deny God's order for creation. They are sending our children the message that anything is okay, and that life-long commitment to one partner of the opposite sex is merely one of many options.

To some readers it may seem that I am advocating hatred toward homosexuals – "gay bashing." Let me assure you that I am not. Every one of us is a sinner and falls short every day, and there is no biblical basis for making homosexuality a worse sin than any other.

To judge a practicing homosexual any more harshly than
another person who has sinned, or to look on him or her
with an attitude of condemnation, is a sin: we know from
the gospels that no sexual sin is so terrible that it cannot
be forgiven or healed (Eph. 2:3–5). Yet we also know that
Jesus hates sin, even though he loves the sinner and wants
to redeem him.

TO AFFIRM HOMOSEXUALITY
IS TO DENY GOD'S CREATIVE INTENT

Homosexual conduct is a sin. It is "against nature," against
God's creative design, and it is a form of self-worship and
idolatry (Rom. 1:26). As a sexual act between two people
of the same gender it is the "very grievous" sin of Sodom
and Gomorrah (Gen. 19:1–29).

In Leviticus 18:22–23, God calls homosexual intercourse
an abomination: "Do not lie with a man as one lies with
a woman; that is detestable." And in Leviticus 20:13 we
read, "The penalty for homosexual acts is death to both
parties. They have brought it upon themselves." Let those
who discount such prohibitions and warnings by explain-
ing that we are now "no longer under the law, but under
grace" then explain why incest, adultery, bestiality, and
human sacrifice are not to be ignored. All of these are
condemned in the very next sentences: "Do not have
sexual relations with an animal and defile yourself with it.
A woman must not present herself to an animal to have
sexual relations with it; that is a perversion."

The New Testament also condemns homosexuality.
In Romans 1:26–28 Paul writes:

> Their women have exchanged natural intercourse
> for unnatural, and their men in turn, giving up natu-
> ral relations with women, burn with lust for one
> another; males behave indecently with males and
> are paid in their persons the fitting wage of such
> perversion.

And in 1 Cor. 6:9–10 Paul writes:

> Do you not know that the wicked will not inherit
> the kingdom of God? Do not be deceived; neither
> the sexually immoral nor idolaters nor adulterers
> nor male prostitutes nor homosexual offenders...
> will inherit the kingdom of God.

Many people reinterpret these Scriptures as condemning
only homosexual rape, promiscuity, and lustful or "unnatural" homosexual behavior by heterosexuals. They
claim that what the Bible condemns is *offensive* homosexual (and heterosexual) behavior. But isn't it clear that
when Paul speaks of "homosexual offenders" he is speaking of the offense of homosexuality itself? If only "offensive" kinds of homosexual acts were evil, then what
about the rest of what Paul mentions in the same pas-
sage: adultery, idolatry, and so forth?

What could be clearer than Paul's words in Romans,
where he calls homosexuality "sinful desire, sexual impurity" and says that it is "degrading and shameful"? Or his

unmistakably sharp words against giving oneself over "to depravity"? (Rom. 1:24–28) Homosexual acts are always perverse, for they always distort God's will for creation. They simply cannot be defended in any way by Scripture. And this is just as true when they take place in a "loving" lifelong relationship. Adulterous heterosexual affairs may also be felt to be loving and may be long-lasting, but that doesn't make them right.

It is typical today to hear people complain about the injustice of holding homosexuals responsible for an orientation or even a way of life that they themselves did not necessarily choose. But this is only an excuse for sin. Whether or not homosexuals are responsible for their sexual orientation has no relevance as to the rightness or wrongness of their behavior. To explain behavior is one thing. To justify it is altogether different.[26]

WHATEVER ITS ORIGIN OR KIND, SEXUAL TEMPTATION CAN BE OVERCOME

The sexual urges of a homosexual can be acute, but so can those of anyone else. All of us are "naturally" predisposed to do what we should not do. But if we believe in God, we must also believe that he can give us the grace to overcome whatever struggles we may have to bear: "My grace is sufficient for you, for my power is made perfect in weakness" (2 Cor. 12:9–10).

In speaking out against homosexuality, we must always remember that even though Scripture condemns homosexual behavior, it never gives us license to condemn the people who engage in it. As Christians we certainly cannot condone the denial of any person's basic human rights, for whatever reason. It is all too easy to forget that the Bible has much more to say about pride, greed, resentment, and self-righteousness than about homosexuality. Nevertheless, we will always resist the agenda of those who try to redefine homosexuality as an "alternative lifestyle" – especially as it affects the legalization of same-sex marriages – as well as efforts to compel religious groups to accept practicing homosexuals as members and even ministers (1 Cor. 5:11).

It is also important to consider the difference between homosexual tendency or "orientation" and an active homosexual lifestyle. Whereas homosexual orientation can arise by means of psychological influences, social environment, and perhaps (according to some scientists) even genetic makeup, an active homosexual lifestyle is a matter of choice. To argue that our culture, family, or genes make us powerless to choose for or against sin is to deny the concept of free will.

Even as an orientation, homosexuality is an especially deep-rooted condition, and those who struggle with it deserve compassion and help. Therefore we always need to be ready to receive the homosexual man or woman into our fellowship and stand with him or her – in patience and love, though also with the clarity that refuses to tolerate continued sexual sinning. Above all, we need to remind those burdened with same-sex attraction of God's original plan for creation, and help them see that neither man nor woman is truly complete without the other.

Whether a struggling homosexual acts on his temptations or not, one thing remains the same: if he turns single-mindedly to Jesus, he can be helped and freed; if he is divided in the depth of his heart, even the most valiant efforts to resist temptation will cramp him in an inner way. Lasting freedom can be found only in decisiveness. Even a furtive glance in the direction of perversion shows that a person is not decided – Jesus says that this is adultery in the heart.

Despite the propaganda of the gay rights activists, we believe that true freedom is possible for every man and woman (Gal. 5:1).[27] No one should pretend that victory is easy. It may not be. For every person who is granted healing, there are dozens more who have to struggle with temptations for years, some for the rest of their lives. Yet is it any different for the rest of us? There cannot be many Christians who have not longed and prayed, seemingly without result, for deliverance from some besetting sin. But we should never doubt that since each of us is created in God's image, there is hope for healing and restoration for each of us (Heb. 9:14). Ultimately, Christ will free us if we give ourselves to him.

WHEN WE FORSAKE GOD, SHAMELESSNESS AND DARKNESS WILL FOLLOW

Less than half a century ago, most people saw homosexual activity as perversion. In society today, it has become accepted as an alternative lifestyle. Frighteningly, there is also increasing acceptance, especially among men, of bestiality (sex with animals) and pedophilia (sex with children). Parents should not be afraid to warn their children about the horror of these perversions, for even though Jesus says that all sin can be forgiven, my experience in counseling men who have engaged in such practices is that they can permanently wound their souls.

Another no less accursed sin is transsexualism – the practice of undergoing a surgical male-to-female or female-to-male sex change. Although unheard of only a few decades ago, this godless practice is gaining momentum across the western world. The enormous cost of these surgeries alone is a crime against humanity when one thinks of the widespread hunger and poverty in the Third World and in our own American ghettos.

What does God think of the shamelessness of our time? In *The Brothers Karamazov*, Dostoyevsky reminds us that "if God does not exist, everything is permissible." Are we not now seeing "everything"? When will we stop to consider the horrifying spirit of rebellion behind our sinfulness and remember God's warnings about his wrath on sinners in the end time? Let us remember the words of Jesus: "You shall reap what you sow." Let us ask God for the mercy of his judgment before it is too late. Let us ask him to shake our deadened consciences, to cleanse us, and to bring us new life.

> The night is nearly over; the day is almost here. So let us put aside the deeds of darkness and put on the armor of light. Let us behave decently, as in the daytime, not in orgies and drunkenness, not in sexual immorality and debauchery, not in dissension and jealousy. Rather, clothe yourselves with the Lord Jesus Christ, and do not think about how to gratify the desires of the sinful nature (Rom. 13:12–14).

CHAPTER 17

THE HIDDEN WAR

You brought me out of the womb; you made me trust in you even at my mother's breast. From birth I was cast upon you; from my mother's womb you have been my God. Do not be far from me, for trouble is near and there is no one to help (Psa. 22:9–11).

Almost seventy years ago, in response to the idea of "modern" family planning, Eberhard Arnold wrote, "In our families we hope for as many children as God gives. We praise God's creative power and welcome large families as one of his great gifts."[28]

What would he say now, in an era where contraception is standard practice and millions of unborn children are legally murdered every year? Where is our joy in children, and in family life? Our thankfulness for God's gifts? Where is our reverence for life and our compassion for those who are least able to defend themselves? Jesus is very clear that no one can enter the kingdom unless he or she becomes like a child.

SEX WITHOUT REGARD FOR
THE GIFT OF LIFE IS WRONG

The spirit of our age is diametrically opposed not only
to the childlike spirit but even to children themselves.
It is a spirit of death, and it can be seen everywhere in
modern society: in the rise of murder and suicide rates,
in the widespread domestic violence, in abortion, the
death penalty, and even euthanasia. Our culture seems
bound on going the way of death, of taking into its own
hands what is God's domain. And it is not only the State
that is at fault.

How many churches sanction the murder of unborn
children under the guise of supporting women's rights?
The sexual "liberation" of our society has sowed tremendous destruction. It is a false liberation built on the selfish
pursuit of satisfaction and pleasure. It wholly ignores
discipline, responsibility, and the real freedom that these
can bring. In the words of Stanley Hauerwas, it mirrors
"a profound lack of confidence that we have anything
worthy to pass on to a new generation...We are willing
our deaths."[29]

It is simply a fact that the vast majority of people today
have no qualms of conscience when the life of a tiny
being is prevented or destroyed. Children, once considered the greatest blessing God can give, are now considered only in terms of their cost: they are a "burden" and
a "threat" to the freedom and happiness of the individual.

In a true marriage, there is a close connection between married love and new life (Mal. 2:15). When husband and wife become one flesh, it should always be with the reverent recognition that through it new life may be formed. In this way the marriage act becomes an expression of creative love, a covenant that serves life. But how many couples today view sex in this way? For most, the pill has made intercourse a casual act, divorced from responsibility and supposedly free of consequence.

As Christians, we must be willing to speak out against the contraceptive mentality that has infected our society. To indulge in sexual pleasure as an end in itself, without regard for the gift of life, is wrong. To close the door to children for any but the gravest considerations is to despise both the gift and the Giver (Job 1:21). When used selfishly, all contraceptive measures, especially permanent surgical methods, are objectionable. This is true even of natural family planning unless there is a good reason not to have a child. Contraception undermines the fulfillment and fruition of two who are one flesh, and because of this we should feel revulsion whenever it is used to consistently avoid the responsibility of bearing children.

Of course, the health and well-being of a mother must always be considered. Sometimes, situations will arise that can only be confronted with earnest prayer and inner searching. What about a mother who is physically or emotionally unable to cope with another pregnancy? Or what should a couple do when a pregnancy must be avoided for medical reasons, when it could be fatal to the mother? Difficult as these questions are, I believe that they can be answered, especially if a couple is willing to turn to trusted elders of the church so that they may face their need with the love and support of others. May God give it that in every situation the right answer is found.

If a drastic step should be necessary, it is the couple who must make the final decision. They alone are responsible to God. At such a point it is especially important for them to turn together in prayer to God and place their uncertainties and needs before him in faith (Mt. 7:7– 8). If we are open to God's leading in every situation, I am confident that he will show us the way. I am hesitant to say more than this.

Of course, what should concern us most is not the question of exceptional moral difficulty, but the pervasive spirit of death that makes new life so unwelcome in so many homes. Everywhere in society today there is a hidden war going on, a war against life. So many little souls wait in vain to be called out of eternity. And of those who are not prevented by contraception from entering the world, how many are callously destroyed by abortion!

TO ABORT ANY CHILD IS TO MOCK GOD

The prevalence of abortion in our society is so great that it makes Herod's slaughter of the innocent tame in comparison. Abortion is murder – there are no exceptions. If there were, the message of the gospels would be incon-

sistent and meaningless. Even the Old Testament makes
it clear that God hates the shedding of innocent blood
(Prov. 6:16–17). Abortion destroys life and mocks God,
in whose image every unborn baby is created.

In the Old Testament there are numerous passages that
speak of God's active presence in every human life, even
while it is still being formed in the womb. In Genesis 4:1
after Eve conceives and gives birth to Cain, she says,
"With the help of the Lord, I have brought a man into
being." She does not say, "With the help of Adam,"
but "with the Lord."

In Psalm 139 we read:

> For you created my inmost being; you knit me to-
> gether in my mother's womb. I praise you because
> I am fearfully and wonderfully made; your works
> are wonderful, I know that full well. My frame was
> not hidden from you when I was made in the secret
> place. When I was woven together in the depths
> of the earth, your eyes saw my unformed body. All
> the days ordained for me were written in your book
> before one of them came to be (Psa. 139:13–16).

Job exclaims: "Did not he who made me in the womb
make them? Did not the same One form us both within
our mother's womb?" (Job 31:15; 10:8–12)

And God said to the prophet Jeremiah, "I knew you
before you were formed within your mother's womb;
before you were born I sanctified you and appointed
you as my spokesman to the world" (Jer. 1:5).

We also read in the New Testament that the unborn are called by God before birth (Gal. 1:15) and that their unique gifts are prophesied while still in the mother's womb. Perhaps one of the most wonderful passages about an unborn child is found in Luke:

> When Elizabeth heard Mary's greeting, the child leaped in her womb. And Elizabeth was filled with the Holy Spirit and exclaimed with a loud cry, "Blessed are you among women, and blessed is the fruit of your womb. And why has this happened to me, that the mother of my Lord comes to me? For as soon as I heard the sound of your greeting, the child in my womb leaped for joy" (Lk. 1:41–44).

Here an unborn child, John the Baptist, the forerunner of Jesus, leaped in Elizabeth's womb in acknowledgement of Jesus, who had been conceived only a week or two before. Two unborn children: one capable of responding to the Holy Spirit, and the other – none other than Christ himself – conceived by the Holy Spirit (Mt. 1:20–21).

Clearly, the idea that a new little life comes into being through something merely physical or biological is a complete falsity. It is God who acts in bringing forth life from the womb (Psa. 71:6). Abortion always destroys this act.

This is why the early church universally rejected abortion, and called it infanticide. The *Didache,* the earliest instruction (100 C.E.) for new Christian converts, leaves no doubt about that: "You shall not slay a child by abortion." And Clement of Alexandria even writes that those who participate in an abortion "wholly lose their own humanity along with the fetus."[30]

Where is the clarity of the church today? Even among so-called Christians, the war of cruelty and death being waged against the innocent unborn children has become a matter of fact, its ghastly horrors and brutal techniques hidden by the mask of medicine and law or even "justified" by every thinkable circumstance.

WHO ARE WE TO JUDGE WHETHER A LIFE IS DESIRABLE OR NOT?

I know it is unpopular to say that abortion is murder. I know that people will say I am removed from reality – that even certain Christian theologians make at least some allowances for abortion. Yet I believe God never does. His law is the law of love. It stands forever, regardless of changing times and changing circumstances: "Thou shalt not kill."

Human life is sacred from conception to death. If we really believe this, we will never be able to accept abortion on any grounds; even the most persuasive arguments about "quality of life" or severe physical deformity or mental retardation will not sway us. Who are we to decide whether or not a little soul should reach the light of day? In God's plan the physically and mentally hindered can be used for God's glory (Jn. 9:1–3). "Who has made man's mouth? Who makes him dumb, or deaf, or seeing, or blind? Is it not I, the Lord?" (Ex. 4:11)

How can we dare to judge who is desirable and who is not? The crimes of the Third Reich – where "good" Nordic babies were bred in special nurseries, while retarded babies, children, and adults were sent to gas chambers – should be warning enough. As Dietrich Bonhoeffer writes, "Any distinction between life that is worth living and life that is not worth living must sooner or later destroy life itself."[31]

Even when the life of a pregnant mother is in danger, abortion is never the answer. In God's eyes, the life of the unborn child and mother are equally sacred. To do evil "so that good may come" is to take God's sovereignty and wisdom into one's own hands (Rom. 3:5–8). In agonizing situations like this, a couple should turn to the elders of their church:

> Is anyone among you suffering? He should keep on praying about it. And those who have reason to be thankful should continually be singing praises to the Lord. Is anyone sick? He should call for the elders of the church and they should pray over him and pour a little oil upon him, calling on the Lord to heal him. And their prayer, if offered in faith, will heal him, for the Lord will make him well; and if his sickness was caused by some sin, the Lord will forgive him (Jas. 5:13–15).

There is great power and protection in the prayer of a united church and in the faith that God's will can be done

for both the life of a mother and her unborn child. In the
end – and I say this with trembling – that is what matters.

WE MUST OFFER ALTERNATIVES,
NOT MORAL CONDEMNATION

As Christians, we cannot simply demand an end to
abortion without offering a positive alternative.
Eberhard Arnold writes:

> Moral philosophers may demand that the sexual life
> be purified by insisting on purity before and in mar-
> riage. But even the best of them are insincere and
> unjust unless they clearly state the actual basis for
> such high demands. Even the destruction of incipi-
> ent life – a massacre of the Innocents intensified a
> thousandfold today – remains unassailable when
> people do not believe in the kingdom of God. The
> supposedly high culture of our day will continue to
> practice this massacre as long as social disorder and
> injustice last. Abortion cannot be combated as long
> as private and public life are allowed to remain as
> they are.
>
> If we want to fight acquisitiveness and the deceit
> and injustice of social distinctions, we must fight
> them in a practical way by demonstrating that a
> different way of life is not only feasible, but actually
> exists. Otherwise we can demand neither purity in
> marriage nor an end to abortion; we cannot wish
> even the finest families to be blessed with the many
> children intended by God's creative powers.[32]

Here the church has failed miserably. There are so many
teenage mothers who are confronted by this question daily,
yet receive no inner guidance, no emotional or economic
support. Many feel they have no other choice than abortion: they have been the victim of sexual abuse; or they
fear an angry boyfriend; or their parents have pressured
them, saying that if they have the baby they can't come
home. Very few young women today are offered viable
alternatives, and almost none of them are pointed to God,
who alone can answer their need.

In speaking out against abortion, we must not forget
that few other sins cause more heartache or anguish of
soul. A woman who has had an abortion suffers great torment of conscience, and her endless pain can be healed
only at the cross – only by finding Christ. Christians need
to feel the immeasurable pain that so many women bear
in their hearts for their lost children. Who of us can cast
the first stone? (Jn. 8:7) Woe to us if we ever become cold
toward a woman who has had an abortion!

God loves the unborn child in a very special way. After
all, he sent us his only son, Jesus, to earth in the form of
a baby, through the womb of a mother. As Mother Teresa
points out, even if a mother turns against her unborn child,
God will not forget him. He has carved each baby in the
palm of his hand and has a plan for each life, not only on
earth but for eternity. To those who would hinder God's
plan, we say with Mother Teresa, "Please don't kill the
child. I want the child. Please give the baby to me."

CHAPTER 18

WHAT ABOUT DIVORCE AND REMARRIAGE?

Everyone who divorces his wife and marries another commits adultery, and he who marries a woman divorced from her husband commits adultery (Lk. 16:18).

Then question of divorce and remarriage is possibly the toughest issue that faces the Christian church in our time. It is harder and harder to find couples who take seriously the words, "What God has joined together, let no one put asunder" – couples who believe that marriage means faithfulness between one man and one woman until death parts them (Mt. 19:6).

A MARRIAGE BOND MAY BREAK, BUT IT CAN NEVER BE DISSOLVED

The majority of Christians today believe that divorce and remarriage are morally and biblically permissible. They argue that though God hates divorce, he allows it as a concession to our sinful condition. Because of our hardness of heart, they explain, marriages can "die" or dissolve. In other words, God recognizes our frailty and accepts the fact that in a fallen world the ideal cannot always be realized. Through God's forgiveness, one can always start again, even if in a new marriage.

But what about the bond that is promised between two and made – whether knowingly or unknowingly – before God? Does God's forgiveness ever mean we can deny it? Does he ever allow unfaithfulness? Just as the unity of the church is eternal and unchangeable, so true marriage reflects this unity and is indissoluble. As the early Christians, I believe that as long as both partners are living, there can be no remarriage after divorce. What God has joined together in the unity of the Spirit is joined together until death parts a couple. Unfaithfulness, whether by one or by both partners, cannot change this. No Christian has the freedom to marry someone else as long as his or her spouse is still living. The bond of unity is at stake.

Jesus is clear that it was because of hard-heartedness that Moses, under the law, allowed divorce (Mt. 19:8). However, among his disciples – those born of the Spirit – hard-heartedness is no longer a valid excuse. Moses said, "Whoever divorces his wife, let him give her a certificate of divorce." But Jesus said, "Everyone who divorces his wife, except on the ground of unchastity, makes her an adulteress; and whoever marries a divorced woman commits adultery" (Mt. 5:31–32). The disciples understood this decisive word of Jesus clearly: "If this is the situation between a husband and wife, it is better not to marry"

(Mt. 19:10). Moses gave allowance to divorce out of sheer necessity, but this hardly changes the fact that from the beginning marriage was meant to be indissoluble. A marriage cannot be dissolved (even if it is broken), neither by the husband who abandons his adulterous wife, nor by the wife who abandons her adulterous husband. God's order cannot be abolished that easily or lightly.[33]

Paul writes with the same clarity to the Corinthians:

> Now to the married I command, yet not I but the Lord: a wife is not to depart from her husband. But even if she does depart, let her remain unmarried or be reconciled to her husband. And a husband is not to divorce his wife (1 Cor. 7:10–11).

He also writes, "A woman is bound to her husband as long as he lives. But if her husband dies, she is free to marry anyone she wishes, as long as he belongs to the Lord" (1 Cor. 7:39). And in Romans he says, "and if she marries another man while her husband is still alive, she is an adulteress" (Rom. 7:3).

Because adultery is a betrayal of the mysterious union between one man and one woman who become one flesh, it is one of the worst forms of deceit. Adultery must always be squarely confronted by the church, and the adulterer must be called to repentance and disciplined (1 Cor. 5:1–5).

THE ANSWER TO A BROKEN BOND
IS FAITHFULNESS AND LOVE

Even if Jesus allows divorce for reasons of fornication
or adultery, it should never be the inevitable result or
an excuse to remarry. Jesus' love reconciles and forgives.
Those who seek a divorce will always be left with the
stain of bitterness on their conscience. No matter how
much emotional pain an adulterous partner causes, a
wounded spouse must be willing to forgive. Only when
we forgive can we ever hope to receive the forgiveness
of God for ourselves (Mt. 6:14–15). Faithful love is the
only answer to a broken bond.

Several times in our communities a married partner
has become unfaithful to Christ and the church, left us,
and subsequently divorced his or her spouse and remarried. Almost every time, the partner left behind has decided to remain in the church, faithful to his or her vows
of membership and of marriage. Though this is naturally
a painful choice – and doubly so when there are children
involved – it is part of the cost of discipleship. If we believe in God, he will give us the strength to hold fast.

At every marriage in our communities, the couple
is asked:

> My brother, will you never follow your wife – and
> my sister, will you never follow your husband – in
> what is wrong? If one of you should turn away from
> the way of Jesus and want to forsake the church
> and the service of God in total community, will you

always place faith in our Master, Jesus of Nazareth,
and unity in his Holy Spirit above your marriage,
also when confronted by government authorities?
I ask you this in the knowledge that a marriage is
built on sand unless it is built on the rock of faith,
faith in Jesus, the Christ.

Although this question may sound hard-hearted to some,
there is deep wisdom in it. In a sense, it is simply a re-
minder of the choice set before each of us who claim to
be disciples: are we ready to follow Jesus at all costs?
Didn't he himself warn us, "Whoever comes to me and
does not let go of father and mother, wife and children,
brothers and sisters, yes, and even life itself, cannot be
my disciple"? (Lk. 14:26)

If a couple takes this warning seriously, it may bring
about separation, but the sanctity of their marriage bond
will actually be protected. The issue here is not only marriage as such, but the deeper bond of unity between two
people united in Christ and his Holy Spirit (1 Cor. 7:15–16).
Whenever a man or woman remains loyal to his or her
partner – no matter how unfaithful that partner may be –
it is a witness to this unity. The faithfulness of God and
his church can always engender new commitment and
hope. We have experienced it more than once that the
faithfulness of a believing partner can lead an unbelieving
partner back to Jesus, back to the church, and back to the
marriage.

TRUE FAITHFULNESS IS NOT MERELY
THE ABSENCE OF ADULTERY

Though God hates divorce, he will also judge every un-
loving or dead marriage, and this should be a warning
to each of us. How many of us have been cold-hearted
or loveless to our spouses at one time or another? How
many thousands of couples, rather than loving each other,
merely coexist? True faithfulness is not simply the absence of adultery. It must be a commitment of heart and
soul. Whenever husband and wife lack commitment to
each other, live parallel lives, or become estranged, separation and divorce lurk around the corner.

It is the task of every church to fight the spirit of
adultery wherever it raises its head. Here I am not only
speaking of adultery as a physical act; in a sense, anything inside a marriage that weakens love, unity, and
purity, or hinders the spirit of mutual reverence, is adultery, because it feeds the spirit of adultery. That is why
God speaks of the unfaithfulness of the people of Israel
as adultery (Mal. 2:10–16).

In the Old Testament, the prophets use faithfulness
in marriage as a picture of God's commitment to Israel,
his chosen people – his bride (Hos. 3:1). In a similar way,
the Apostle Paul compares marriage to the relationship of
unity between Christ, the bridegroom, and his church, the
bride. Only in the spirit of these biblical images can we
clearly consider the question of divorce and remarriage.

When a church does nothing to nurture the marriages of its own members, how can it claim innocence when these marriages fall apart? When it shies away from testifying that "what God has joined together, no one should put asunder," how can it expect its married members to remain committed for life?

In considering these questions, there are two pitfalls we must avoid. First, we can never agree to divorce; second, we must never treat those who suffer its need and pain with legalism or rigidity. In rejecting divorce, we cannot reject the divorced person, even if remarried. We must always remember that though Jesus speaks very sharply against sin, he never lacks compassion. But because he longs to bring every sinner to redemption and healing, he requires repentance for every sin. This is also true for every broken marriage.

Clearly, we must never judge. At the same time, however, we must be faithful to Christ above everything else. We must embrace his whole truth – not just those parts of it that seem to fit our needs (Mt. 23:23–24). In our church community, therefore, no baptized member may divorce and remarry if a former spouse is still living; likewise, no divorced and remarried couple may become full members while continuing to live in a marriage relationship. Remarriage compounds the sin of divorce and precludes the possibility of reconciliation with one's first partner. We stand for lifelong fidelity in marriage. No other stand is consistent with real love and truthfulness.

WITH GOD, ALL THINGS ARE POSSIBLE

Naturally, if divorce is to be avoided, the church must offer its members guidance and practical support long before their marriages collapse (Heb. 10:24; 12:15). Even if there are only slight indications that a marriage is at risk, it is best to be honest and open about it. Once a couple drifts too far apart, it may take space as well as time for them to find each other's hearts again. In a situation like this, as in one where a partner has become abusive, temporary separation may be necessary. Especially when this is the case, the church must find concrete ways to help both partners – first in seeking repentance and then in finding the mutual trust and forgiveness necessary to restore the marriage.

It is sad that in today's society, faithfulness is so rare that it has come to be seen as a "heroic" virtue. Shouldn't it be taken for granted as the bedrock of our faith? (Gal. 5:22) As followers of Christ, shouldn't each of us be willing to hold firm through thick and thin, until death, to Christ, to his church, and to our husband or wife? Only with this resolve can we hope to remain faithful to our marriage vows.

The way of discipleship is a narrow way, but through the cross anyone who hears the words of Jesus can put them into practice (Mt. 5:24). If Jesus' teaching on divorce and remarriage is hard, it is only because so many in our day no longer believe in the power of repentance and forgiveness. It is because we no longer believe that what

God joins together can, by his grace, be held together;
and that, as Jesus says, "With God, all things are possible."

Nothing should be too hard for us when it is a require-
ment of the gospel (Mt. 11:28–30). If we look at Jesus'
teaching on divorce and remarriage in this faith, we will
see that it is one of great promise, hope, and strength. It is
a teaching whose righteousness is much greater than that
of the moralists and philosophers. It is the righteousness of
the kingdom, and it is based on the reality of resurrection
and new life.

CHAPTER 19

THEREFORE
LET US KEEP WATCH

The wedding of the Lamb has come, and his bride has made herself ready. Fine linen, bright and clean, was given her to wear...Blessed are those who are invited to the wedding supper of the Lamb! (Rev. 19:7–9)

Despite the shamelessness and promiscuity of our time, we believe that purity and faithful love are still possible today. Even if the established churches have neglected to proclaim the message that sexual happiness is possible within the commitment of marriage alone, we are still certain of its truth. There is no question that many people today have a deep longing for purity and faithfulness. But longing is not enough. Only when we are willing to follow and obey the leading of the Holy Spirit, cost what it may, can we experience its great blessings in our daily lives. Do we believe deeply enough in the power of the Spirit? Are we willing to let God transform our hearts so completely that he turns our lives upside down? (Rom. 12:2)

THE STRUGGLE FOR PURITY
DEMANDS DAILY RESOLVE

All of us know temptation, and all of us have given in to temptation. All of us have failed at one time or another – in our relationships at work and at home, in our marriages, and in our personal lives. The sooner we face that, the better. Yet we can take comfort, even if we struggle with ups and downs, and even if our moments of victory are followed by moments of doubt. Even Jesus was tempted, and he was tempted in every way we are (Heb. 4:15). With his help we can find the purity that protects us from every temptation. James says, "Blessed is the one who stands firm in temptation" (Jas. 1:12). What matters here is the deepest will of our heart – the will that speaks within us whenever we come before God in prayer.

As we struggle to be faithful, it is of greatest importance that our entire will is decided for purity. A divided heart will never be able to stand (Jas. 1:6–7). But willpower alone cannot bring about singlemindedness. If we work ourselves into an inner frenzy, even if we manage to keep our head above water, we will soon tire out and sink. Only if we surrender to Jesus can the power of his grace fill us and give us new strength and resolve.

In combating the spirit of our age, we must fight not only against the obvious sins of fornication, deceit, murder, and so on, but also against apathy and fear. Hardly anyone will say that he is against faithfulness and love, or opposed to justice and peace, but how many of us are ready to fight for these things in word and in deed? The

spirit of our time has dulled us with such a deathly com-
placency that we are usually content to look the other
way. But if we do not speak out against the evil of our
time through the actions of our lives, then we are just as
guilty as those who sin deliberately. We must all change,
and we must start with ourselves.

Where are there people like John the Baptist today?
Where are the "voices in the wilderness" crying out for
repentance, conversion, faith, and a new life? John's message was simple: "Repent, for the kingdom of God is at
hand!" He was not afraid to confront anyone, including
the leaders of his day. He even confronted King Herod on
his adulterous marriage, saying, "It is not lawful for you to
have her" (Mt. 14:3–4). Perhaps most significant, though,
he called to account the devout and religious, the "good"
people: "You brood of vipers! Who has warned you to
flee from the wrath to come? Therefore bear fruits of
repentance" (Mt. 3:7–8).

IN THE FIGHT FOR GOD'S KINGDOM, GOOD DEEDS ARE NOT ENOUGH

In the Gospel of Matthew, Jesus says to his disciples, "The
harvest is plentiful but the workers are few" (Mt. 9:37).
How much truer is this today! So many people long for
the freedom of Christ but remain chained to their sins. So
few people dare to stick out their necks. The task is great.

Most of us have good intentions; we earnestly desire
to do good deeds. But that is not enough. We dare not
forget that the fight for God's kingdom is not just against

human nature: we are dealing with something far more powerful, with powers and principalities (Eph. 6:12), and with the destructive, demonic spirit that John calls the "beast from the abyss" (Rev. 9:11).

This beast holds sway over every country and every government, and its mark is to be found everywhere in our day: in the disappearance of lasting friendship and community, in the oppression of the poor, and in the exploitation of women and children. It is to be seen in the wholesale murder of the unborn and the execution of the imprisoned. Most of all, it is to be seen in the lonely desperation of so many millions of people.

We are living in the end time. It is the last hour (1 Jn. 2:18). We must be on the watch continually if we are not to fall under judgment in the last hour of temptation. We need to seek the inner strength and courage to speak up for God and his cause, even if no one seems willing to hear us.

Jesus' parable of the ten virgins should be a warning and a challenge to all of us. Jesus is not speaking here about the lost world on the one hand and the church on the other: all ten of the women in the story are virgins, and all of them are preparing to meet him. He is challenging the church:

> The kingdom of heaven will be like ten virgins who took their lamps and went out to meet the bridegroom. Five of them were foolish and five were wise. The foolish ones took their lamps but did not take any oil with them. The wise, however, took oil

in jars along with their lamps. The bridegroom was a long time in coming, and they all became drowsy and fell asleep.

At midnight the cry rang out, "Here's the bridegroom! Come out to meet him!" Then all the virgins woke up and trimmed their lamps. The foolish ones said to the wise, "Give us some of your oil; our lamps are going out."

"No," they replied, "there may not be enough for both us and you. Instead, go to those who sell oil and buy some for yourselves." But while they were on their way to buy the oil, the bridegroom arrived. The virgins who were ready went in with him to the wedding banquet. And the door was shut.

Later the others also came. "Sir! Sir!" they said, "Open the door for us!" But he replied, "I tell you the truth, I don't even know you."

Therefore keep watch, because you do not know the day or the hour (Mt. 25:1–13).

ARE WE WILLING TO DEMONSTRATE THAT A NEW WAY EXISTS?

We cannot merely run from the challenge of sin. Instead, we must live in active protest against everything that opposes God. We must openly fight everything that cheapens or destroys life, everything that leads to separation and division. But we must also recognize that protest alone, which often leads to violence, is not sufficient. To simply renounce the world, reject marriage, or refuse all pleasure would be fruitless.

We must demonstrate that a new way exists and show
the world a new reality, the reality of God's righteousness
and holiness, which is opposed to the spirit of this world.
We must show with our lives that men and women can
live lives of purity, peace, unity, and love wherever they
dedicate their energies to working for the common good;
and not only by creating spiritual community, but by
building up a practical life of sharing. Above all, we must
witness to the power of love. Each of us can give our
lives to others in the service of love. That is God's will
for humankind (Jn. 13:34–35).

Certainly, wherever God's will is lived out, it will be
misunderstood and seen as provocation (1 Pet. 4:4).
Two thousand years have not made our present world
any more tolerant of Jesus' message than the world of
his time. Those who are unwilling to accept his way will
always be resentful and even vindictive toward those
who witness to it, and a clash is inevitable (Jn. 15:18–20).
But if we who claim to follow Christ are afraid to live out
his commands because we fear persecution, who will do
it? And if it is not the task of the church to bring the darkness of the world into the light of Christ, whose is it?

Our hope is in God's coming kingdom, which is the
wedding feast of the Lamb. Let us wait faithfully for that
day. Every word we say, everything we do, should be
inspired and influenced by our expectation. Every relationship, every marriage, should be a symbol of it. Jesus,
the bridegroom, expects a bride prepared and waiting for
him. But when he comes, will we be ready? Will we be

"a radiant church, without stain or wrinkle"? (Eph. 5:27)
Or will we be full of excuses? (Lk. 14:15–24)

We must never be afraid of the ridicule and slander
our witness will bring on us. What grips us and drives
us should be God's future – the wonderful future of his
kingdom – not the present "realities" of human society.
It is God who holds the final hour of history in his hands,
and each day of our lives should be a preparation for
that hour

NOTES

[1] Johann Christoph and Christoph Friedrich Blumhardt, *Now is Eternity* (Rifton, NY: Plough, 1976), 13.

[2] Thomas Merton, *New Seeds of Contemplation* (New York: New Directions, 1972), 180.

[3] Quoted in Eberhard Arnold, *Love and Marriage in the Spirit* (Rifton, NY: Plough, 1965), 102.

[4] Friedrich E. F. von Gagern, *Der Mensch als Bild: Beiträge zur Anthropologie*. 2nd ed. (Frankfurt am Main: Verlag Josef Knecht, 1955), 32.

[5] Quoted in Hans Meier, *Solange das Licht Brennt* (Norfolk, CT: Hutterian Brethren, 1990), 17.

[6] *Der Mensch als Bild*, 33–34.

[7] Dietrich Bonhoeffer, *Ethics* (New York: Macmillan, 1975), 19.

[8] *Der Mensch als Bild*, 58.

[9] *Love and Marriage in the Spirit*, 152.

[10] J. Heinrich Arnold, *Discipleship* (Farmington, PA: Plough, 1994), 42.

[11] Eberhard Arnold, *Inner Land* (Rifton, NY: Plough, 1976), 55–56.

[12] Dietrich Bonhoeffer, *The Cost of Discipleship* (New York: Macmillan, 1958) 95–96.

[13] Cf. Peter Riedemann, *Confession of Faith* (1540), (Rifton, NY: Plough, 1974), 98.

[14] *Discipleship*, 160–161.

[15] Ernst Rolffs, ed., *Tertullian, der Vater des abendländischen Christentums: Ein Kämpfer für und gegen die römische Kirche* (Berlin: Hochweg, 1930), 31–32.

[16] Jean Vanier, *Man and Woman He Made Them* (New York: Paulist, 1994), 128.

[17] Friedrich von Gagern, *Man and Woman: An Introduction to the Mystery of Marriage* (Cork, Ireland: Mercier, 1957), 26–27.

[18] Johann Christoph and Christoph Friedrich Blumhardt, *Thoughts About Children* (Rifton, NY: Plough, 1980), 29.

[19] *Thoughts About Children*, 9.

[20] *Discipleship*, 169.

[21] *Discipleship*, 177–178.

[22] Dietrich Bonhoeffer, *The Martyred Christian: 160 Readings* (New York: Collier Macmillan, 1985), 170.

[23] Eberhard Arnold, *The Early Christians* (Rifton, NY: Plough, 1972), 18.

[24] *The Wall Street Journal*, Dec. 10, 1993.

[25] "Church report accepts cohabiting couples." *The Tablet*, June 10, 1995.

[26] Thomas E. Schmidt, *Straight and Narrow? Compassion and Clarity in the Homosexual Debate* (Downers Grove, IL: InterVarsity, 1995), 131–159.

[27] In his book *Straight and Narrow?*, especially pp. 153–159, Thomas E. Schmidt includes a discussion of various programs and organizations for men and women seeking a way out of the homosexual lifestyle. See the bibliography.

[28] Eberhard Arnold, *God's Revolution* (Farmington, PA: Plough, 1992), 151.

[29] Stanley Hauerwas, *Unleashing the Scripture: Freeing the Bible from Captivity to America* (Nashville: Abingdon, 1993), 131.

[30] Michael J. Gorman, *Abortion and the Early Church: Christian, Jewish, and Pagan Attitudes in the Greco-Roman World* (New York: Paulist, 1982), 47–62.

[31] *Ethics*, 164.

[32] *Inner Land*, 155.

[33] If divorce and remarriage are never justified, then why does Jesus allow marital unfaithfulness as an exception? (Mt. 5:32,19:9) Without going into great detail, two things can be said. First, in Jesus' day a husband was required, by Jewish law, to divorce an adulterous wife (e.g. Mt. 1:19). Thus, in Mt. 5:32, Jesus is saying that a man who divorces his unfaithful wife (which the law required he do) is not responsible, by this action, for her adultery. In any other kind of divorce, however, he is the culpable one; the adulterer. When we come later to Mt. 19:9, then, the exception of marital unfaithfulness should be read to apply to divorce only and not to remarriage.

WORKS CITED

Arnold, Eberhard. *The Early Christians*. Rifton, NY: Plough, 1972.

_____. *God's Revolution*. Farmington, PA: Plough, 1992.

_____. *Inner Land*. Rifton, NY: Plough, 1976.

_____. *Love and Marriage in the Spirit*. Rifton, NY: Plough, 1965.

Arnold, J. Heinrich. *Discipleship*. Farmington, PA: Plough, 1994.

Blumhardt, Johann Christoph and Christoph Friedrich. *Now is Eternity*. Rifton, NY: Plough, 1976.

_____. *Thoughts About Children*. Rifton, NY: Plough, 1980.

Bonhoeffer, Dietrich. *The Cost of Discipleship*. New York: Macmillan, 1958.

_____. *Ethics*. New York: Macmillan, 1975.

_____. *The Martyred Christian: 160 Readings*. New York: Collier Macmillan, 1985.

"Church report accepts cohabiting couples." *The Tablet*, June 10, 1995.

Gagern, Friedrich E. F. von. *Man and Woman: An Introduction to the Mystery of Marriage*. Cork, Ireland: Mercier, 1957.

_____. *Der Mensch als Bild: Beiträge zur Anthropologie*. 2nd ed. Frankfurt am Main: Verlag Josef Knecht, 1955.

Gorman, Michael J. *Abortion and the Early Church: Christian, Jewish, and Pagan Attitudes in the Greco-Roman World*. New York: Paulist, 1982.

Hildebrand, Dietrich von. *Purity: The Mystery of Christian Sexuality*. Steubenville, OH: Franciscan University Press, 1989.

Hauerwas, Stanley. *Unleashing the Scripture: Freeing the Bible from Captivity to America*. Nashville: Abingdon, 1993.

Meier, Hans. *Solange das Licht Brennt*. Norfolk, CT: Hutterian Brethren, 1990.

Merton, Thomas. *New Seeds of Contemplation*. New York: New Directions, 1972.

_____. *No Man is an Island*. New York: Harcourt Brace Jovanovich, 1955.

Riedemann, Peter. *Confession of Faith* (1540). Rifton, NY: Plough, 1974.

Rolffs, Frnst, ed. *Tertullian, der Vater des abendländischen Christentums: Ein Kämpfer für und gegen die römische Kirche*. Berlin: Hochweg, 1930.

Schmidt, Thomas E. *Straight and Narrow? Compassion and Clarity in the Homosexual Debate*. Downers Grove, IL: InterVarsity, 1995.

Vanier, Jean. *Man and Woman He Made Them*. New York: Paulist, 1994.

The Wall Street Journal, Dec. 10, 1993.

FOR FURTHER READING

Arnold, Eberhard. *Children's Education in Community.* Rifton, NY: Plough, 1976. Short selections on the practical and spiritual education of children.

_____. *God's Revolution.* Farmington, PA: Plough, 1992. Topically arranged excerpts from the author's talks and writings on community, marriage, the family, children, and the church.

Arnold, Eberhard. *Love and Marriage in the Spirit.* Rifton, NY: Plough, 1965. Talks and essays on the meaning of faith as the basis for a true Christian marriage.

_____, and Thomas Merton. *Why We Live in Community.* Farmington, PA: Plough, 1995. Inspirational thoughts on the basis, meaning, and purpose of Christian community.

Arnold, J. Heinrich. *Discipleship.* Farmington, PA: Plough, 1994. Thoughts on following Christ in the daily grind, topically arranged. Includes sections on sex, love, marriage, parenting, and celibacy.

_____. *Freedom From Sinful Thoughts.* Rifton, NY: Plough, 1976. Spiritual insights on the struggle to overcome personal sins and temptations.

Bloesch, Donald G. *Is the Bible Sexist?* Westchester, IL: Crossway, 1982. A sane and sober approach to the volatile issue of feminism in the church that is both sensitive to women's concerns *and* solidly grounded in the Bible.

Blumhardt, J. Christoph and Christoph F. *Thoughts About Children.* Rifton, NY: Plough, 1980. Practical pastoral insights on raising, guiding, and caring for children.

Bonhoeffer, Dietrich. *Life Together.* New York: Harper and Brothers, 1954. A time-honored manifesto on one the most essential aspects of being: solitude, interaction, and community.

Chesterton, G.K. *Brave New Family*. San Francisco: Ignatius, 1990. Prophetic and insightful essays on love, sex, marriage, gender roles, children, and the institution of the family in western society.

Clapp, Rodney. *Families at the Crossroads*. Downers Grove, IL: InterVarsity, 1993. A thoughtful discussion on the role of the church in family life from a biblical perspective.

Cornes, Andrew. *Divorce and Remarriage*. Grand Rapids, MI: Eerdmans, 1993. The most thorough biblical and pastoral treatment of this difficult subject to date.

Fromm, Erich. *The Art of Loving*. Reflections on the definition and meaning of love.

Gagern, Friedrich E. F. von. *Difficulties in Married Life*. New York: Paulist, 1964. Thoughtful advice from an experienced Catholic psychiatrist.

——————. *Man and Woman: An Introduction to the Mystery of Marriage*. Cork, Ireland: Mercier, 1957. Sex education with an emphasis on reverence as the key to a healthy sexuality.

Gorman, Michael J. *Abortion and the Early Church*. New York: Paulist, 1982. A readable and concise treatment on the early church's stand against abortion.

Groeschel, Benedict J. *The Courage to Be Chaste*. New York: Paulist, 1985. A helpful and encouraging book that addresses issues facing all single men and women.

Hildebrand, Dietrich von. *Purity: The Mystery of Christian Sexuality*. Steubenville, OH: Franciscan University Press, 1989. A masterful work on the meaning of purity – and Christ's call to a pure life.

——————. *Man and Woman: Love and the Meaning of Intimacy*. Manchester, NH: Sophia Institute, 1992. A lucid discussion of the nature of love and the mystery of sexuality.

Kierkegaard, Søren. *Purity of Heart is to Will One Thing*. New York: Harper and Row, 1956. A classic series of addresses on individual responsibility and undivided devotion to God.

Laney, J. Carl. *The Divorce Myth*. Minneapolis: Bethany House, 1981. A compassionate but uncompromising challenge to the institutions of divorce and remarriage, from a biblical perspective.

Mow, Anna B. *The Secret of Married Love*. Philadelphia: J.B. Lippincott, 1970. An insightful look at marriages based on romantic love as opposed to those built on the foundation of spiritual unity and self-giving love.

Neuer, Werner. *Man and Woman in Christian Perspective*. Wheaton, IL: Crossway, 1991. A biblical discussion of the commonalities (and differences) between men and women.

Schmidt, Thomas E. *Straight and Narrow? Compassion and Clarity in the Homosexuality Debate*. Downers Grove, IL: InterVarsity, 1995. A frank but uncompromising scriptural treatment of homosexuality.

Hutterian Brethren, eds. *A Straight Word to Kids and Parents: Help for Teen Problems*. Ulster Park, NY: Plough, 1987. Readable but thought-provoking pieces on everything from drug and alcohol abuse to peer pressure, from suicide and homosexuality to TV addiction, written by men and women who have struggled with these issues.

Vanier, Jean. *Community and Growth*. New York: Paulist, 1989. A bestselling collection of readings, topically arranged, calling for a radical turn from the disintegration and divisiveness of contemporary society to love, mutual support, and community.

_____. *Man and Woman He Made Them*. New York: Paulist, 1984. Reflections and advice on sexuality and human relationships from the founder of the L'Arche communities.

ABOUT THE BRUDERHOF

D espite all that is wrong in our society, we must witness to the fact that God's spirit is at work in the world today. God still calls men and women away from the systems of injustice to his justice, and away from the old ways of violence, fear, and isolation to a new way of peace, love, and brotherhood. In short, he calls us to community. In this sense, we – the brothers and sisters of the Bruderhof communities in the United States and England – wish to share some thoughts on our response to this call.

INNER BASIS

The basis of our communal life is Christ's teachings in the Sermon on the Mount and throughout the New Testament, especially those concerning brotherly love and love of enemies, mutual service, nonviolence and the refusal to bear arms, sexual purity, and faithfulness in marriage.

We have no private property but share everything in common, the way the early Christians did as recorded in the book of Acts. Each member gives his or her talents, time, and efforts wherever they are needed. Money and possessions are voluntarily pooled, and in turn each member is provided for and cared for. We meet daily for meals, fellowship, singing, prayer, and decision making.

WORK

Our life is a joyful one, as full of the sounds of song and play as of work. We earn our living by manufacturing and selling Community Playthings (a line of play equipment and furniture for children) and Rifton Equipment for People with Disabilities. Our work is far more than a business venture, however. From wash-

ing clothes and dishes to assembling products in our work-
shops, it is a practical expression of our love for one another.

FAMILY AND CHILDREN

Although many of our members are single adults, the family is
the primary unit of our community. Children are a central part
of our life together. They need a place where they can truly be
children. Parents are responsible for educating their children to
be accountable and caring, but the teachers of our daycare and
school, as well as the entire community, support with guidance
and encouragement. In this way, problems can be managed,
burdens and joys shared.

Babies and small children receive daily supervision in our
Children's House, after which they attend our community
school (K–8). Teenagers attend public high school before mov-
ing on to university, college, or technical/vocational training.
Some young adults find work in mission service projects and
return with valuable knowledge and experience.

Our invalid and elderly members are a treasured part of the
community. Whether participating in the communal work (even
if only for a few hours a day) or being visited at home by children, they enrich our life with their vitality and experience.

HISTORY

Our movement has struggled forward against the currents of
contemporary society. Miraculously, we have been held together through times of physical danger and spiritual decline.
In 1920, Eberhard Arnold, a well-known theologian, lecturer,
and writer, left wealth, security, and an increasingly public
career in Berlin and moved with his wife and children to

Sannerz, a tiny German village, where they founded a small
community based on the practices of the early church.

Despite persecution by the Nazis and the turmoil of World
War II, the community survived. After expulsion from Germany
in 1937, the movement settled in England, though with the out-
break of World War II a second migration was necessary, this
time to South America. For twenty years the community lived
in a remote part of Paraguay, the only country willing to accept
our multinational group. In 1954 a branch community was
started in the United States.

THE PRESENT

In 1961 the Bruderhof closed its communities in Paraguay and
all members moved to Europe and the United States. Today
there are six communities in the northeastern U.S. and two in
southeastern England. We are insignificant in numbers, yet we
believe our task is of utmost importance: to follow Jesus' teachings in a society that has turned against him.

OUTREACH

Mission has always been a vital focus of our activity, though not
in the sense of trying to "save" people or gain members for our
church. Far more important to us are the connections we make
with others who serve a cause greater than themselves, no
matter what their label. At a local level, we are involved in
voluntary ambulance and fire service, prison ministry, and other
community service projects. In the last few years we have made
contacts further afield, and recent journeys have taken us to
Russia, Europe, Iraq, Israel, New Zealand, Haiti, Africa, South
and Central America, Korea, and Japan.

VISION

We come from many countries, races, and walks of life, but we are all brothers and sisters. Guests are welcome at all our Bruderhofs, but they are advised that our life is not a utopian escape from the world. Life in community demands self-denial, honesty, accountability, and the willingness to confront problems and work them out face-to-face.

We are well aware of our human weaknesses as individuals and as a community, yet we believe that it is possible to live out Jesus' clear way of love, freedom, and truth in deeds. With Eberhard Arnold we affirm: "This planet, the earth, must be conquered for a new kingdom, a new social order, a new unity, a new joy. This joy comes to us from the God who is the God of love, who is the spirit of peace and of unity and community. This is the message Jesus brings. And we must have the faith and the certainty that his message is valid still today."

THE PLOUGH PUBLISHING HOUSE

The Plough Publishing House of the Bruderhof communities sells books about our communal life and the vision of radical Christianity that inspires it. We also publish a small periodical, *The Plough*, with articles on the urgent issues of today: social and economic justice, nonviolence, discipleship, the family, education, and community.

Sample copies or a subscription are available free on request, though we welcome donations to meet costs. For more information about our communities, our books, and our magazine, call in the USA: 1-800-521-8011 or 412-329-1100 in the UK: 0800-269-048 or +44 (0) 1580-881-003

For more information about the Bruderhof
or to arrange a visit, write or call:

Woodcrest Bruderhof
Rifton, NY 12471
Tel: 914/658-8351

Pleasant View Bruderhof
Ulster Park, NY 12487
Tel: 914/339-6680

Catskill Bruderhof
Elka Park, NY 12427
Tel: 518/589-5103

Deer Spring Bruderhof
Norfolk, CT 06058
Tel: 203/542-5545

New Meadow Run Bruderhof
Farmington, PA 15437
Tel: 412/329-8573

Spring Valley Bruderhof
Farmington, PA 15437
Tel: 412/329-1100

Darvell Bruderhof
Robertsbridge, E. Sussex
TN32 5DR, U.K.
Tel: +44 (0) 1580-881-003

Beech Grove Bruderhof
Nonington, Kent
CT15 4HH, U.K.
Tel: +44 (0) 1304-842-980

The author with Pope John Paul II, New York City, October 1995

"I was glad to deliver your manuscript, *A Plea for Purity*, to the Holy Father. He was very happy for this ecumenical gesture and, more than that, for the contents and for the harmony of moral conviction that springs from our common faith in Christ. Such conviction will inevitably arouse hatred, even persecution. The Lord has predicted it. But with him we must continue in trying to overcome evil through good."

From a letter, Joseph Cardinal Ratzinger
to Johann Christoph Arnold, December 1995

OTHER TITLES FROM PLOUGH

SALT AND LIGHT by Eberhard Arnold. Talks and writings on the transformative power of a life lived by Jesus' revolutionary teachings in the Sermon on the Mount.

GOD'S REVOLUTION by Eberhard Arnold. Topically arranged excerpts from the author's talks and writings on the church, community, marriage and family issues, government, and world suffering.

LOVE & MARRIAGE IN THE SPIRIT by Eberhard Arnold. Talks and essays on the importance of faith as a basis for meaningful and lasting Christian relationships.

INNER LAND by Eberhard Arnold. Timeless essays on the "inner land of the invisible" where men and women may find strength and courage to follow God's call in today's world.

WHY WE LIVE IN COMMUNITY by Eberhard Arnold, with two interpretive talks by Thomas Merton. Inspirational thoughts on the basis, meaning, and purpose of community.

THE EARLY CHRISTIANS by Eberhard Arnold. Letters and sayings of the early church in the words of its own members. Includes material from a variety of contemporary sources.

DISCIPLESHIP by J. Heinrich Arnold. A collection of thoughts on following Christ in the daily grind, topically arranged. Includes sections on love, humility, forgiveness, leadership, gifts, community, sexuality, marriage, parenting, illness, suffering, mission, salvation, and the kingdom of God.

FREEDOM FROM SINFUL THOUGHTS by J. Heinrich Arnold. Spiritual insights on the struggle to overcome personal sin and temptation, and on the freedom of a Christ-centered life.

THE GOSPEL IN DOSTOYEVSKY An introduction to the "great God-haunted Russian" comprised of passages from the *Brothers Karamazov, Crime and Punishment,* and *The Idiot.*